Suddenly the Storm

PAUL SLABOLEPSZY

WITS UNIVERSITY PRESS

Published in South Africa by:

Wits University Press
1 Jan Smuts Avenue
Johannesburg, 2001
www.witspress.co.za

First published 2017

978-1-77614-092-3 (Print)
978-1-77614-093-0 (PDF)

Application to perform this work in public and to obtain a copy of the play
should be made to: Dramatic, Artistic and Literary Rights Organisation
(DALRO), P O Box 31627, Braamfontein, 2017. No performance may be
given unless a licence has been obtained.

Edited by Pat Tucker
Proofread by Hazel Cuthbertson
Cover image by Suzy Bernstein
Cover design by Fire and Lion, South Africa
Typesetting by Fire and Lion, South Africa

For Bob …
For the journeys travelled …
And those still to come

Contents

Foreword

Paul Slabolepszy is one of South Africa's best-known and most popular and prolific playwrights, his works having been performed in the United Kingdom, the United States, Germany, France, Australia, Sweden, Denmark and the Middle East. His body of work is extraordinary, with more than 30 plays written in close on 40 years. In addition, he has written numerous screenplays, television and radio plays.

My 34-year director/playwright association with Paul, which started in 1982 at the Market Theatre with *Saturday Night at the Palace* and has stretched to nearly a score of stage, television and film productions, has been a rare blessing in my career. I have had the privilege of seeing him develop as a playwright. As a close family friend I have watched him balance his career as an actor with his writing and performing and his role as husband and father. In this country it is difficult to make a living in the arts and almost impossible to support a family by just writing plays. I believe that this constant financial battle shaped the course of his plays, determining the subject matter of many of his works.

Saturday Night at the Palace was Paul's first major success as a playwright and it certainly put me on the map as a theatre director, with our production touring South Africa for two years before travelling to Ireland, Sweden and having a six-week season at the Old Vic theatre in London.

The play established a style which has become a hallmark of Paul's writing: quintessentially South African characters in situations that are initially highly amusing but gradually become more serious, more moving and, very often, tragic. At the height of the apartheid era this recipe had an exceptional impact, drawing thousands of people into the theatre with the expectation of great entertainment, yet having them leave with more than a little uneasiness about what they had witnessed and how it reflected on their lives in those troubled times.

Subsequent successes of plays such as *Boo to the Moon, Making Like America, Travelling Shots, Smallholding, The Eyes of their Whites* (co-written with David Kramer) and *Pale Natives,* all of which I have had the pleasure of directing, had the same tragi-comic power, with indelible characters forcing us to look at ourselves and our country in a new light.

Interspersed with these works were enormously successful comedies and farces, focusing on Paul's other great love – sport. *Under the Oaks, Tickle to Fine Leg, It's Just not Cricket, Life's a Pitch* (cricket); *Over the Hill, Heel Against the Head* (rugby), *Once a Pirate* (soccer); *Whole in One, Not the Big Easy* (golf) and *Running Riot* (ultra-marathon running) were all extremely popular across the length and breadth of South Africa. Paul has sometimes been criticised for writing these so-called 'inconsequential comedies'. True, perhaps they have less to say about the human condition in our country, and may not have the relevance of *Saturday Night at the Palace, Pale Natives* or *Suddenly the Storm,* but they are highly entertaining stories with razor sharp depictions of South Africans. More importantly, they were successful financially, enabling Paul to make a living from theatre at a time when it was exceptionally difficult to do so.

Several of the works cited above, along with plays such as *The Return of Elvis du Pisanie, Fordsburg's Finest, Crashing the Night* and *For Your Ears Only*, were also vehicles for Paul's wonderful talent as an actor. He has won numerous Best Actor awards, in particular for his extraordinarily moving performance as Eddie in *The Return of Elvis du Pisanie.* In addition, Paul wrote several roles for his lifelong friend and acting colleague, the late Bill Flynn, and the two became household names as a comic duo in movie versions of *Heel Against the Head* and *Running Riot.*

Paul has very graciously dedicated *Suddenly the Storm* to me 'For the journeys travelled … And those still to come'. I am greatly moved by this honour. It means even more to me that he has done so with this play, because I believe that it closes a circle that began with *Saturday Night at the Palace.*

'*Palace*' was written by a young playwright at the start of his career and he entrusted the birth of his baby to a young director at the start of his own career. '*Suddenly*' could not have been written without the wealth of life experience the playwright has gathered over nearly 40 years and I could not have contributed as much to the process without the working relationship that has been built over a lifetime's friendship and collaboration. There are few things as satisfying as offering constructive criticism to someone who instantly 'gets' what you are saying and turns it into a positive development. The relationship between playwright and director is a delicate one and, in our case, it has been a joyful, extremely productive association that has grown stronger with the years.

Saturday Night at the Palace was, to my mind, Paul's best and most important play, until *Suddenly the Storm*. The former made a deep impression on a very wide range of South African citizens at a time when most forms of anti-apartheid protest were stifled by the government. Now, more than 30 years later, we still regularly encounter people who tell us how the play affected them and has continued to live with them right up to the present day.

Suddenly the Storm deals with the way the wounds inflicted by apartheid on so many people from different backgrounds are still hurting today. Paul has an unerring knack of tapping into the psyche of ordinary people and with *Suddenly the Storm* he touches audiences who recognise that even 40 years after 16 June 1976 – the day the Soweto Uprising began – there is still a great deal of healing to be done. I believe that time will prove that this play is as important a reflection of this, as '*Palace*' was of its time.

Like Paul, I started my career as an actor. I mention this because both of us understand actors and acting and this has been immensely useful to us throughout the delicate process of writing, moulding and staging our theatre productions. From the outset we have always been on the same page when assessing how characters speak and move and emote; and this was the first of many elements that made our playwright/director/actor relationship so smooth and productive.

Suddenly the Storm took several years to reach the stage and I had the privilege of watching it develop. Paul kept me abreast with his ideas as he wrote a play called *Guarding Mrs Gumede*, a process that took a good five years. It was a two-hander about a security guard who is called out one night to guard a fearful Mrs Gumede in her home. During the course of a stormy night their respective lives are explored and examined and it is revealed that the divorced security guard's marriage had 'made a tsunami look like a ripple in a birdbath'.

The play was eventually completed to the point where it was ready to be submitted to a national festival for consideration. We both knew it was a powerful piece and were confident that it would be accepted. To our surprise, the play was turned down. We were gutted. In the aftermath, Paul happened to tell his daughter, Frances, that he had written the play as a two-hander, mainly to make it financially viable. He felt he should have simply written the three-hander he had originally had in mind. Frances asked him why he shouldn't go ahead and write the play he wanted to, forgetting about 'financial constraints'.

Encouraged by this advice, Paul literally tore *Guarding Mrs Gumede* to shreds and began, painstakingly, to reassemble his now brand-new story, in the process bringing to life the 'missing' wife. The play that emerged was far more exciting and incisive than the original – audiences could now witness the 'tsunami' of a marriage rather than hearing about it from only one of the protagonists. *Suddenly the Storm* was born.

What I subsequently received from Paul was a play that was already several degrees more complex than a usual first draft because the original story, complex in itself, now had several more layers and intriguing twists and turns added into the mix.

The process of working with Paul on this virgin script was incredibly exciting. I immediately saw that he had created a play that could be looked at in many ways: a thriller, an historically relevant play about South Africa, a drama, and a heart-rending love story that was, at the same time, fresh and universal.

I consider it my duty as a director to point out exciting possibilities lying hidden in a new script and encourage Paul to develop them, while occasionally persuading him to 'kill his darlings', as we shape each play for staging. With *Suddenly the Storm* all the material was there, but each time he presented me with a new draft I would point out further possibilities and he would go away even more enthused and return a few days later with a fresh draft and the process would be repeated. In all, I think Paul wrote some half-dozen drafts.

The creation process became even more exciting when we moved into the rehearsal stage; what I like to call moving 'from page to stage'. Paul says that a play isn't really a play until it is performed. My job is to assist him with that transformation. Play texts are sometimes like radio plays, where the sense is largely carried in the dialogue. When the play is performed the audience can observe the live performers, and this immediately makes it more opulent. When a character is saying one thing, he may actually be conveying something else physically, and it is my job to explore and enhance those intriguing situations.

As I worked on *Suddenly the Storm* with our magnificent cast of Paul, Charmaine Weir-Smith and Renate Stuurman, we became aware that it was particularly rich in the possibility of telling different stories physically from those being told in the dialogue: what we call 'subtext'. When Shanell is rattling on excitedly about the new stuff she has purchased, how much is she hiding the watery guts she is experiencing as she anticipates Dwayne's reaction? When she is apologising to Dwayne for shouting at him, is she actually trying to distract him from seeing incriminating details on her cellphone? When alone and unobserved, how does she apply her perfume?

As a director, one of my tasks in rehearsals is to match the rich, revealing dialogue with the physical. For instance, when Shanell offers her black guest a drink, would she think about using a water glass rather than a wine glass? Would she wash the glass? How much wine would she pour into it? There is great satisfaction in seeing an audience picking up the unspoken story, the subtext, especially when it becomes integrated into the published text for future generations. The sense of fulfilment a director, writer and cast get from rehearsing a new play for the first time, from exploring the possibilities and developing the situation and characters, is something that only those who have experienced it can fully appreciate.

Paul has no peer when it comes to natural South African dialogue. It is no accident that the characters in several of his plays come from far-flung areas of our country. Paul is the champion of the downtrodden. His characters often find that life has passed them by and they are left wondering what went wrong along the way. They are characters we can't help laughing at, but ultimately we also understand that they are people created by a country with a unique history, and we invariably empathise with them.

To my mind, Paul had written a very real play with *Suddenly the Storm*, so my instinct was to match that gritty reality in the staging. We hired Greg King, a designer renowned for making brilliantly real and detailed sets. My job then was to push that sense of realism even further, contriving to have real welding, actual angle-grinding, authentic running water, physical raindrops and realistic lightning and thunder that totally envelop the audience. Attention to detail is everything. Where would Dwayne keep the key to Jonas's locker? Why would Dwayne keep Jonas's blanket folded so neatly on the car seat? How would Namhla handle a bloody handkerchief?

The casting can obviously make or break a play. The actors are an integral part of the development of a virgin play in the rehearsal process. We were blessed in finding Charmaine Weir-Smith and Renate Stuurman, great actresses able to match Paul's brilliance. The characters have to be very real and recognisable.

Dwayne has been kicked in the guts by life. He has to be inherently angry to the point of being disliked by the audience, until the story reveals exactly why he is so angry and unhappy and we empathise with him.

Shanell cannot understand how or why she has disappointed her husband. She has to be the comic relief in the play, no mean task for an actress in a role that has to be totally believable and not a caricature. She, too, must be understood as the person this country has made her.

Namhla's life has also been shaped by apartheid. She has to be the rock, the calm eye of the storm, around which the husband-and-wife tsunami roars. If the director has good actors who are attuned to the process, the development of strong characters comes more easily, to the benefit of future actors who may play them.

Paul has incorporated some of the rehearsal detail into the final draft of the script, where he feels it has become a vital part of the story that is now being told on the stage. I consider that a gift and a privilege to me, the initial director, in bringing the play to life for the very first time. I hope that subsequent directors will also add their insights.

Playwriting is a hard business, especially in a country where we are not afforded the luxury of 'try-outs' in the provinces before being exposed to the harsh reality of the main theatres' audiences and critics. I have witnessed Paul and other playwrights spending months and years writing and producing a play only to have it die soon after birth because of an unfavourable response or lack of exposure in the media. In tackling a new play, the director accepts the challenge of giving it the best chance of a long, successful life. One first-time theatregoer called the experience of watching a live play 'like watching Life in 4D'. I am acutely aware of my responsibility in coaxing Paul's deeply-considered and skilfully-crafted stories into 4D life.

Pale Natives is a savagely funny and powerful story of five white men fearful of their future in the 'new' South Africa. Like Dwayne, Shanell and so many of Paul's characters, they have reached the stage of their lives when they realise that things haven't turned out the way they expected. When we first staged *Pale Natives* in 1994 it starred, among others, Paul and Bill Flynn, and it won several Best Actor, Best Play and Best Production awards. We staged it again in 2015 with a new generation of actors and it was equally uproarious and powerful and once again won awards for its actors and director … it had become an important reflection of the turbulence that marked the birth of South African democracy. I am confident that, like *Pale Natives* and many of Paul's other plays, *Suddenly the Storm* will stand the test of time and be a significant work for future generations of actors and audiences.

Bobby Heaney
Johannesburg
February 2017

Glossary[1]

afdak	corrugated iron roof, lean-to [Afr]
bakkie	pick-up truck [Afr]
boggerol	buggerall, nothing
bok	keen, up for it [Afr]
boma	a cattle or animal enclosure [South African, originally East African]
bome	trees [Afr]
bossies	crazy [Sl, orig Afr]
china [my]	friend [Sl]
chommie	friend, mate [Sl]
doff	dopey, thick, stupid [Sl, orig Afr]
doos	box, cunt [Afr]
doos-wyn	box-wine [Afr]
doosagtige	cunt-like [Afr]
dwang	trouble, strife [Sl]
finish-and-klaar	end-of-story, over-and-done-with [Afr]
fliek	a movie, the movies [Afr]
gaaning-aan	carrying on [Afr]
gagga	urgh, distasteful [Afr]
gat	hole, arsehole [Afr]
gemors	mess, filth [Afr]
getik	touched in the head, a screw loose [Afr]
gomgat	arsehole, scumbag [Afr]
gooi	throw, go for it [Afr]
graze	food, 'chow' [Sl]
haregat	stingy, stuck-up [Afr]

Note:

1 Afr – Afrikaans; Sl – slang

ibheshu	skins, traditional garb at Zulu weddings [isiZulu]
jislaaik, jeez-laaik-it	toned down 'Jesus' [Afr]
jol	a good time, play [Afr]
jong	chap, man [Afr]
kak	shit, crap [Afr]
khakibos	type of bush, a weed [Afr]
klap	smack, 'clap' [Afr]
kleilatte	a game in which a ball of mud or clay is flicked off a springy twig [Afr]
kotch	vomit [Sl]
KZN	KwaZulu-Natal
laaitie	young boy, kid [Afr]
lapa	open-air entertainment area [siNdebele]
larney	smart, fancy [Sl]
lekker	nice [Afr]
los [it]	leave [it] [Afr]
maar	but [Afr]
mahala	free, for nothing [isiZulu]
mal	mad, crazy [Afr]
mishoop	pile of manure [Afr]
moer	smash[ed], bash, hit [Afr]
moersa	massive, huge [Afr]
mos	of course, only [Afr]
muti	African medicine [isiZulu]
nogal	also [Afr]
nooit	never, no way [Afr]
oke (oukie)	'bloke' [Sl]
plak	case or story [Afr]
poep	shit, fart [Afr]
pondok	shack, hovel [Afr]
sangoma	'witch-doctor', traditional healer [isiZulu]
sis	yeugh! [Afr]
sjambok	whip made of hide [Malay]
sjoe	phew! [Sl]

skeef	squint, off kilter [Afr]
skeem	scheme, think [Sl]
skinner-stories	gossip [Afr]
skoonveld	vanished, disappeared [Afr]
skraal	thin, scrawny [Afr]
skriks-for-niks	afraid of nothing [Afr]
skyf	smoke, cigarette [Afr; Sl]
slag	slaughter, kill, murder [Afr]
slash	piss, urinate [Sl]
sommer	just, merely [Afr]
sowaar	certainly, for sure [Afr]
stiffies	too bad, sad for you [Sl]
stompie	used cigarette butt, fragment [Afr]
tjanking	chirping, whining, going on and on [Afr]
toetie	full amount [Afr]
ukuphi, wendoda	where are you, friend? [isiZulu]
umlungu	racially 'white' person [isiZulu]
uyangizwa na	can you hear me? [isiZulu]
veldskoene	leather lace-up shoes [Afr]
verdwyn	disappear, lose [Afr]
voetsek	get lost, fuck off [Afr]
vrot	drunk, rotten [Afr]
waai	go away, leave [Afr]
wag-a-bietjie bome	thorn trees, 'wait-a-bit trees' [Afr]
windgat	braggart, big deal [Afr]
woes	extremely angry [Afr]
yassas	softer version of 'Jesus' [Afr]

NAMHLA (Renate Stuurman, left) and SHANELL (Charmaine Weir-Smith, right): "No, you know … starts off all friendly and if you lucky it's over in two ticks. They don't play along, out he goes with this blimmen baseball bat, his gun, and I'm thinking, Ooo, gonna, is he ever coming back? But he always does." (Photograph Suzy Bernstein).

DWAYNE (Paul Slabolepszy, left) and SHANELL (Charmaine Weir-Smith, right): "It's our … what-joo-callit, man! Our *ship*! Our ship has finally come in. After all these years … the struggles … the mess we still sit with thanks to that useless Harry bladdy Serfontein!" (Photograph Suzy Bernstein).

As SHANELL (Charmaine Weir-Smith) moves away to return to bed, DWAYNE (Paul Slabolepszy) reaches out and takes her hand, pulling her back and holding her fiercely to him. (Photograph Suzy Bernstein).

A play in five scenes

Directed originally by Bobby Heaney

CHARACTERS

DWAYNE … sixty-plus
SHANELL … pushing fifty
NAMHLA … forty

Launched to coincide with the 40th anniversary of the Soweto Uprising of 1976, *Suddenly the Storm* had its world premiere at the Barney Simon at Johannesburg's Market Theatre on 7 June 2016. The production was directed by Bobby Heaney, with set and costume design by Greg King and lighting design by Wesley France.

Dwayne was played by Paul Slabolepszy, Shanell by Charmaine Weir-Smith and Namhla by Renate Stuurman.

The play was subsequently performed with the same cast at the Auto & General Theatre on the Square, Nelson Mandela Square, Sandton, from 27 October 2016.

The action takes place in the office-cum-workshop of a security gate and fence works on the outer reaches of the Far East Rand, the home of an ageing former policeman and his much younger wife.

The time is early summer 2016.

Scene 1

A rambling, ramshackle house on the plots, early evening.

The set comprises an untidy, cluttered office adjacent to a workshop [part of which we see through a double-door opening in the rear wall]. There is a large desk [SR], creaking beneath the weight of grubby files and ledgers. The swivel chair behind the desk looks as though it has been attacked by a pack of rabid hyenas. The single back seat of a minibus taxi serves as a sofa; a neatly-folded old Pep Stores blanket is draped over it. In front of the seat, a cloth-covered crate serves as a coffee table. On a tatty notice board on the wall behind the desk there is a garish calendar, designs for metal gates, signs and memos. Against the back wall is a tiny washbasin, with an old bar-type mirror above it. Beside it is a table on which stands a decrepit miniature fridge. A tall, narrow, battered, padlocked metal locker stands at the entrance to the workshop. It is festooned with Orlando Pirates memorabilia – an old team photo and decals. There are various makeshift shelves against other walls, all weighed down with accumulated bric-a-brac. In the middle of the wall [SL] there is a window, in front of which hangs an ancient venetian blind, permanently semi-open. An archway leads to the interior of the house [downstage SR] and a small vestibule leads to the [front] exterior door [downstage SL]. A metal bucket stands centre stage, midway between the desk and the car seat.

As pre-set lighting slowly begins to fade, Johnny Clegg's 'Your Time Will Come' [from Heat, Dust and Dreams] kicks in

*over the sound system. The song continues as lights fade up
on the empty office. Presently,* DWAYNE, *a tanned, weather-
beaten individual in his early sixties enters, breathing
heavily [SL]. A real East Rand Cowboy, he wears an old
brown leather bomber jacket, checked shirt, well-worn
denim jeans and veldskoene. He packs a revolver at his hip
and wields a battered, bloodied baseball bat. Stopping just
inside the doorway, he picks up a piece of newspaper and
wipes the bat clean, tossing it onto the car seat. Reaching for
the bucket, he places it beneath the tiny basin. He heads for
the fridge-table and, uncapping his Klipdrift brandy bottle,
notices his hand is shaking rather badly. He pours himself a
hefty triple shot and takes a gulp, carrying the glass across
to the desk. The music fades out, ending with the rumble of
a retreating thunderstorm. Setting the glass down he hauls
out fat wads of R200 and R100 notes [ten thousand Rand's
worth] from various pockets. Dropping the money onto the
desk he digs around for a key, unlocks the top drawer of the
desk and drops the money into it. He speed-dials a number
on the cordless desk phone.*

DWAYNE [*into phone, matter-of-factly*]: Ja, howzit. Mission
    accomplished … ten-Gs on the nose. [*A beat. He
    snorts disdainfully.*] Ja, well – this is Africa, China –
    what can I say? [*A beat.*] Sweet. Whenever you like
    [*tosses the phone down*].

    Giving the phone the middle finger DWAYNE *begins
    searching for a job sketch. Unable to locate it, he thrusts
    his head into the workshop and calls out gently …*

DWAYNE: Hey, Jonas!

About to call out again he stops short. Shaking his head, he looks heavenward …

DWAYNE [*wistfully*]: uYangizwa na?

Beat.

uKuphi, wendoda?

He continues his slow, methodical search for the security gate sketch … crooning the first three lines of the second verse of the song 'Blueberry Hill' under his breath … he locates the sketch and ambles off, softly singing the first two lines of the last verse …

No sooner has DWAYNE disappeared into the workshop than a dolled-up-to-the-nines, heavily made-up blonde in her late forties appears in the interior [SR] archway. Mutton-dressed-as-lamb, she is the epitome of Brakpan Chic. SHANELL COMBRINK was First Princess in a Miss West Rand Beauty Pageant in the late 1980s and somewhere in her head she is still back there, still desperately holding on. Clutching her handbag, she kisses her pendant and then heads for the small, grubby mirror above the basin for a last-minute make-up check.

DWAYNE emerges from the workshop as she crosses. He gawks at her flashy get-up.

SHANELL [*paying him scant attention*]: How did it go?
DWAYNE [*with a dismissive grunt*]: Ja-OK.

He heads for his desk, picking up his unfinished brandy.

SHANELL [*eyes on the mirror*]: Listen, I'm going into town. Me and Candice Wolmerans, we gonna catch a fliek. Don't wait up. [*Beat.* DWAYNE *is preoccupied.*] Hashtag, just saying.

Beat.

DWAYNE [*quietly, perching on the edge of the desk*]: You won't believe what I just did.

SHANELL [*still looking in the mirror, spots some facial blemish*]: Oh, flip, look at this now!

DWAYNE: Stuck my head in the workshop and called out his name.

SHANELL: For heavensake, Dwayne. Get yourself a mirror you can see something in, man! [*She sorts out the blemish.*] OK, lekker – that's me. [*She digs into her handbag for car keys.*] Where's my bladdy …? Urgh!

DWAYNE [*preoccupied*]: There's nothing left.

SHANELL: Ag-no, man!

She digs in vain.

DWAYNE: Sebokeng.

Beat.

SHANELL: What you tjanking on about now?

DWAYNE: Took a drive down to Sebokeng this afternoon.

SHANELL: What the hell for?

She resumes digging into her handbag.

DWAYNE: His shack's gone. Skoonveld.

SHANELL [*irate*]: This is bladdy *ridiculous!*

Thoroughly irritated, SHANELL *scours the shelves.*

DWAYNE: Every last piece a' zinc, plank, nail, you name it … *voeff!*

SHANELL: Ja, well – what did you expect?

DWAYNE: It was his home.

SHANELL: Please …! [*She points to the locker.*] That bashed-up blimmen locker was more his home than any shack in Sebokeng! *That* locker and this excuse for a bladdy sleeping couch [*She is flustered.*] You seen my …? Losing my *mind* here!

DWAYNE: We gotta organise that headstone.

SHANELL: What …? [*She turns on him.*] Are you *mad?* Where you gonna get the money now all of a sudden to get him a blimmen headstone?

DWAYNE: It's a cultural thing.

SHANELL: You know how much those things *cost!*

DWAYNE: Jonas had just one wish …

SHANELL: For heavensake, Dwayne, Jonas is dead! You buried him! Like he's gonna know now he's got a headstone stuck over his head or not!

DWAYNE: I made a promise.

SHANELL: Oh, nice. Yes. You and your promises. You promised me a rose garden, sunshine, and what did I get? Dust, khakibos and a pondok on the plots half-a-million miles from the nearest bladdy shopping mall! [*She heads towards the alcove.*] Not surprised everything gets lost in this place, look at it … like a dumpsite! A rotting municipal bladdy landfill! Sis! *Gagga!*

She disappears into the house through the alcove to look for her keys. In the meantime, DWAYNE has removed his jacket and placed it over the back of his chair. He moves slowly to the battered metal locker and examines the padlock that secures it. He looks about … drifts across to a shelf and rummages through pieces of metal offcuts. Selecting a metal bar, he heads back to the locker. Inserting the bar between the flap and the padlock, he gives it a couple of smacks before the lock breaks. He tosses down the metal bar and swings open the locker.

SHANELL [*off, not happy*]: Ag, for a crying in a bladdy bucket, man! You put anything anywhere in this place, the bladdy things grow legs!

DWAYNE carefully, lovingly, removes the contents of the locker. There is a well-used pair of safety goggles, a faded blue overall and heavy-duty gloves. Finally, he locates a hessian bag. Old and dusty, it has obviously remained hidden for a long time. He carefully carries the heavy bag to the makeshift coffee table.

Sitting down, he opens the bag to reveal an object that takes his breath away … the large rhino horn before him is a wonderful specimen indeed.

He turns the horn over in his hands with a mixture of shock, awe and barely-controlled excitement. The sound of jingling keys is heard off [SR] through the alcove. He quickly puts the horn down, covering it with the hessian bag.

SHANELL [*speaking as she enters, crosses to look out through the venetian blinds. She is anxious*]: Ja, listen, that big fancy car came past *again* today, hey ... tinted windows. Third time this week orreadt. Slows down and then speeds off. [*Grimly.*] Prolly checking us out. Checking to see who's at home, who's not. [*She is keen to be on her way.*] Okay ... like I said ... don't wait up.

DWAYNE looks almost catatonic, eyes staring ahead, his hands covering the bag.

SHANELL [*noticing the empty locker*]: I see you got his locker open. You can chuck all that stuff out now.

She heads for the door.

DWAYNE's thousand-mile stare unsettles her.

SHANELL: You orraight?
DWAYNE: Hundred percent.

Beat.

SHANELL: What you got there?
DWAYNE: It's nothing ... it's just ...

> *SHANELL approaches. DWAYNE knows she's onto him. She peels the hessian away, revealing the rhino horn. At first glance she is clueless as to what it is.*

SHANELL [*recoiling in horror*]: Urgh! Ag, no sis, man! No wonder your bladdy office stinks like the abattoirs. Throw that thing away!
DWAYNE: Ja, no, OK ... [*willing her to leave.*] Listen ... enjoy the fliek.
SHANELL: OK. I will. See you when I see you. [*She exits. A beat. She returns slowly.*] Wait a minute, is that a ...? Is that what I *think* it is?

DWAYNE: You gonna be late for your movie.

SHANELL: Don't come with your kak now! [*She sits on the car seat, looking at the horn.*] Good God …! How much is a thing like that, like … *worth*?

Beat.

DWAYNE [*still awestruck*]: Rhino horn on the black market, you looking at anything up to two, two-and-a-half.

SHANELL: Thousand?

DWAYNE [*derisively*]: How's your head? You getik?

SHANELL: Well, how must I know?

DWAYNE: Talking millions.

SHANELL: Oh, my God, no … not two *million*? Two million *Rand*? [*She jumps up, showing euphoria and disbelief in equal measure.*] I can't … I actually, I'm … I'm *finish!* [*She suddenly stops, concerned.*] What if it's a fake? You sure it's not a …

DWAYNE: It's not a fake.

SHANELL [*mind racing*]: But how on earth did he …? Where did he …? Did he *steal* it? What if he stole it? What if he stole it from one of those poachers?

DWAYNE: For fucksake, man! Shaddap!

SHANELL: Don't tell me to shut up! We've had something worth a fortune sitting in this dirty, stinking locker heaven knows how long, and you just …

DWAYNE: That locker belongs to Jonas.

SHANELL: *Belonged* to Jonas! Jonas is dead!

DWAYNE: So you keep reminding me.

SHANELL: So what you saying to me here?

DWAYNE: I dunno.

SHANELL: It's our … what-joo-callit, man! Our *ship!* Our ship has finally come in. After all these years … the struggles … the mess we still sit with thanks to that useless Harry bladdy Serfontein!

DWAYNE [*quietly*]: Yassas!

SHANELL [*euphoric*]: It's a gift, don't you see? From Jonas! *His* gift to *us*!

DWAYNE: Us … who too haregat to give him a headstone.

There is a long pause. They both stare at the precious find on the coffee table.

SHANELL: So what we do now?

DWAYNE looks at his wife, his mind in turmoil. The haunting sound of Simunye [eGolgotha] breaks the silence … the choral voices swell … growing louder as the lights slowly fade to scene-change mode.

Scene 2

Mid-afternoon, next day.

Lights fade up as the choral voices continue, then slowly fade out.

The bright sunlight through the blinds makes neat horizontal patterns across the empty office. Off, through the open door to the workshop, we hear the sound of a welding machine, the buzzing noise is unmistakeable. With each buzz an eerie blue light strobes the workshop. This stop-start process goes on for a short while. Then the sound ceases completely.

Looming in the doorway and entering from the workshop is a startling apparition. DWAYNE *resembles a creature from the lost lagoon in his huge welding mask and thick leather apron. He heads for the fridge, opens it, takes out a bottle of cold water and drinks deeply. He glances at Jonas's locker, has a thought about the horn and moves to his desk, picking up the telephone.*

He reaches for a small, tatty notebook. Flipping through it he locates the number he is after. Halfway through dialling he hears the familiar sound of his wife's car returning and pulling up outside. He drops the phone onto the desk and ambles back into the workshop.

No sooner has DWAYNE *disappeared than* SHANELL *enters through the downstage 'exterior' door. She is dressed in an over-the-top flashy outfit that appears to have been newly acquired and breathes heavily under the weight of several large, bursting, plastic shopping bags she carries in both hands.*

SHANELL [*calling out, tentatively*]: Dwayne!

> *She places the shopping bags down beside the car seat and adjusts her new dress, tugging it down. Off, in the workshop, the welding sounds have given way to the sound of a heavy hammer on metal … a few lusty blows.*

> SHANELL *digs into one of the bags and takes out the first in a set of matte-painted metal kitchen containers. The quintessence of kitsch, it reads UGARS. She places it on the coffee table, stepping back to admire it. She moves towards the workshop, keen for her husband to see her new purchases.*

SHANELL [*excited*]: Dwayne!
DWAYNE [*off, distracted*]: Ja, what?

> *The phone on the desk begins to ring and* SHANELL *answers it.*

SHANELL [*into the phone*]: Far East Gate & Fence, how may I help you? Sorry? Oh, hullo, Mrs … [*listens, frowns*] … barber of what? OK, fine, he'll call you back [*nodding*] ja, ja … soon as he can. Bye-ee.

> SHANELL *replaces the receiver as* DWAYNE *enters from the workshop, tape measure in hand. He is no longer wearing his welding gear and his grubby T-shirt is sweat stained.*

DWAYNE [*not looking at her*]: Was that the Stuck Record?
SHANELL: Mrs de Freitas. Wants to know why her security gate's not finish.
DWAYNE [*rolling his eyes*]: Happy days.

SHANELL: She's *woes* with you, jong.

DWAYNE: Stiffies.

> *He has crossed to the window in order to measure a metal gate placed beside it.*

SHANELL: What's a Barber of Civil?

DWAYNE: Huh?

SHANELL: Her gate-thingy. She called it Barber of Civil.

> *DWAYNE's eye has been caught by something outside the window, across the street. Throughout what follows, his attention will be fully focused on that.*

DWAYNE: Barber a' *Seville*. It's a design.

SHANELL: Named after a barber?

> *DWAYNE, still looking out, puts the tape measure down.*

SHANELL: Who now goes and names burglar bars after a bladdy hairdresser?

DWAYNE [*split-focus*]: It's *Spanish.*

SHANELL: If it's Spanish, why not just sommer call it Spanish? [*She mutters, grimly.*] Hell. *People!* In *my* world, a spade is a spade, finish-and-klaar.

DWAYNE: Would that we all lived in your world, Shanell.

> *Her preening and cavorting in her new dress has failed to attract her husband's attention so she goes for the direct approach.*

SHANELL: So …? [*Brightly.*] How do you like …?

DWAYNE [*his gaze focused firmly outside now*]: Ja.

SHANELL: Hey. Dwayne … [*indicating herself.*] I'm over here! [*Beat. Then she gets it.*] What you looking at?

DWAYNE: Serious bunch a' horses under *that* bonnet.

SHANELL *is at his side in an instant, peering out through the blinds along with him.*

SHANELL [*aghast*]: Oh, my fuck! It's that *car* again!

DWAYNE: Hot off the showroom floor.

SHANELL: Oo, shit! Someone's getting out … [*A beat, she's stunned.*] It's a *girl*! [*She ogles, transfixed.*] She's not some maid looking for work, that's for sure. [*Beat. She watches keenly.*] Maybe she's got something to do with Jonas?

DWAYNE: Driving wheels like *that?*

SHANELL [*snapping*]: This is not funny, Dwayne. It's giving me the heebies! [*She gasps suddenly.*] What if she's coming round here alla' time 'cos she knows about the rhino horn?

DWAYNE: Nobody knows bugger-all about that horn.

SHANELL: Yes, but …

DWAYNE: We been through this … four-five years stuck in that locker. Minimum!

SHANELL [*urgently*]: Oh, look! She's leaving. She's driving off!

DWAYNE: Sweet.

He turns to move back to the workshop.

SHANELL: Sweet? That's all you can say?

DWAYNE has spotted her shopping bags and the containers beside the car seat.

SHANELL: Least you could do is go tune her …

DWAYNE [*transfixed by her purchases, livid*]: And now?

SHANELL: Ask her what's her plak.

DWAYNE: What is this!!?

SHANELL: Oh, this. [*She perks up.*] Lemme show you …
for the kitchen … [*She takes the UGARS tin from the
shelf.*] Ta-raaaah! [*Awaits response.*] You get it?

DWAYNE [*fuming*]: No, I don't.

SHANELL [*indicating, reading*]: 'UGARS'! [*She is
triumphant.*] It's Sugar! Clever, hey? [*Like a child
showing off her 'things' she whips out a tin marked
'ASLT'.*] Look … see here … Salt! Back-to-front …
wrong-way-round. [*She frowns.*] Actually, woulda'
been nicer if it was 'TALSA'. [*She considers this.*]
Although, hold on – TALSA's two A's, hey? Ag,
anyway, you know what I mean … [*She parades yet
another container that reads 'LOURF'.*] You get like
the whole set. Sugar … Flour … Rice … full-toetie!
[*She laughs.*] Like the lady in the shop said, it's
dyslectic-proof! [*She giggles excitedly again.*] Oh, and
then … here, look here …

A punch-drunk DWAYNE *can only stare in disbelief,
taking the blows one by one.*

SHANELL: This was a real bargain. [*She produces a shawl
triumphantly.*] Pashmina! Raw silk! Can use it as a
stole, a scarf … and then osso as a kind of, like …
throw. You know what's a throw?

Beat.

DWAYNE: Have you completely lost your mind?

SHANELL: Ja, OK, orraight. I went a bit mal, I know, but
I'm enjoying myself. Those bladdy banking people can
finally go jump. And, ja … to hell with that clapped-

out blimmen Daihatsu! I want a Peugeot, a silver
Peugeot … or maybe blue! That sorta' twinkly blue
that like sparkles when it's wet.

DWAYNE: Fuck me, George. You skeem this is how it
works?

SHANELL: We gonna sell this place. We gonna go down to
Ballito, and …

DWAYNE: And what? Champagne? Caviar?

SHANELL: Just think! No more Chateau de Doos Wyn!

DWAYNE: Yassas!

He spins away.

SHANELL: What's stopping us? We got the money now!

DWAYNE: We got zilch! Zero!

SHANELL: Ja, but as soon as you get somebody to buy that
…

DWAYNE: For fucksake, woman, you do not go waltzing
down the drag, the first oke you meet: 'Hey, you
wanna score a rhino horn, hows-about three bar?'

SHANELL: I know it's not like that.

DWAYNE: There's a whole process here. Gotta find a
Contact. A Go-to-Guy who's not gonna turn around
and stick a knife in your back.

SHANELL: What about someone like Stavros?

DWAYNE [*wild laugh*]: I call Stavros, next thing I got every
gom-gat schnaai-merchant from the Cape to bladdy
Cairo smashing my door down!

SHANELL: So how far you got orready? [*DWAYNE looks
away.*] You haven't even yet started!?

DWAYNE: I'm working on it.

SHANELL: You working on it?

17

DWAYNE: Slowly-slowly, catch a monkey.

SHANELL [*dead serious*]: I'm telling you one thing, Dwayne. You better get this right. You better score what's coming to us or s'true's bob, I'm outa' here.

DWAYNE [*crossing to fetch the gate*]: Ah, gimme a break, Shanell. You been on your way outa' here ever since Abraham parted the Red bladdy Sea.

SHANELL: Moses parted the Red Sea and I'm parting with you, better believe it!

DWAYNE: Ja, well, why don't you just bugger off right now, man! [*He picks up the gate and heads for the workshop.*] Cut your losses and sommer waai!

SHANELL [*ultra-defiant*]: Like hell, I will!

DWAYNE [*indicating the shopping bags*]: And while you're at it, take all this shit with you!

He disappears into his workshop bearing the security gate.

SHANELL [*apoplectic, shouting in the direction of the workshop*]: Fuck you, Dwayne Combrink! Fuck you! Fuck-fuck-fuck-fuck-fuck!

Muttering to herself, on the brink of tears, she gathers all her purchases and lugs them off into the house, exiting through the interior arch.

From the workshop comes the sound of a heavy hammer against a metal bar ... several blows ... then complete and utter silence ... the world has stopped.

NAMHLA, *an elegant black woman, fortyish, stylishly dressed, Afro-chic, enters tentatively through the front entrance. She holds on tightly to her expensive designer handbag, one hand inside it, as she moves into the office, looking carefully about.*

She displays no emotion as she surveys this alien place, scanning the notice board in the manner of a fiction writer or an investigative journalist in search of 'juicy' material.

DWAYNE, unaware of her presence, enters from the workshop and crosses to fetch a new angle-grinding disc from a shelf near the front door. As he swings around NAMHLA quickly slips her hand out of her handbag and their eyes lock. It is as though they are both turned to stone.

DWAYNE [*dead calm*]: Afternoon.
NAMHLA [*equally calm*]: Good afternoon.

The tableau again … staring. When next they speak, they speak simultaneously.

DWAYNE: How did you get in?
NAMHLA: The gate was open, and …

DWAYNE is clearly flustered, while she shows absolutely no emotion.

DWAYNE: I was just wondering how you …

He indicates the front door.

NAMHLA: The security gate was open. I thought that …
DWAYNE: It's OK.

A beat before, again, they speak simultaneously.

NAMHLA: I wasn't aware that …

DWAYNE: It's not a train smash …

> *DWAYNE chuckles now, self-consciously, while her expression remains unchanged.*

DWAYNE: This is getting a bit strange.

> *NAMHLA's gaze unsettles DWAYNE and he appears mesmerised. Before it gets any weirder SHANELL barges in through the alcove lugging all her packages.*

SHANELL [*grimly resolved*]: Right. Okay. You want me to take all this stuff back I do it on one condition. [*She stops dead in her tracks on spotting their guest.*] Oh, my goodness! [*She recognises the woman-from-the-fancy-car.*] It's you!

DWAYNE [*grimly*]: You left the gate open.

SHANELL: I forgot. With all the packets, I was …

DWAYNE: Bossies, ja.

> *There is an awkward pause … stalemate … NAMHLA has not taken her eyes off DWAYNE, who is clearly unsettled. It is left to SHANELL to make the next move.*

SHANELL [*flustered, to the visitor*]: Is there anything we can do for you?

> *Beat.*

NAMHLA [*eyes fixed on DWAYNE*]: I'm not entirely sure.

> *DWAYNE backs off, reversing into his workshop. Is it the job at hand or his need to flee this woman and her unrelenting gaze? SHANELL half follows him.*

SHANELL: Dwayne? [*Her apprehension is growing.*]
Dwayne!

DWAYNE bangs away briefly in the workshop … a pause … SHANELL is all at sea.

SHANELL [*flustered*]: Are you now a friend of Jonas?
NAMHLA: I beg your pardon?

She casts a keen gaze around the office.

SHANELL: Jonas passed away.
NAMHLA: My condolences.
SHANELL: He died like five weeks ago.
NAMHLA: I'm sorry.
SHANELL: Ja. [*Beat.*] So you not like a relative or like, someone who …?
NAMHLA: I'm not, no.
SHANELL: Oh. [*Beat.*] I like your shoes.
NAMHLA [*distracted*]: Hm?
SHANELL: Your shoes. They very nice.
NAMHLA: Thank you.
SHANELL: I'm very partial to shoes. [*She smiles vacuously.*]
A person can look at a person's shoes, and there's … quite a lot you can tell. [*Beat as she indicates the shopping bags.*] Excuse all the … er … ja. How does it go? Shop 'til you drop, hey.

Her attempt at levity goes down like a cup of cold sick. SHANELL is rescued by the familiar sounds of industry coming from the workshop. The clank of hammer on metal is a blessed distraction. Then the banging stops.

SHANELL [*glancing towards the workshop*]: You got to forgive my husband. He's got a customer wanted

21

something yesterday. It's like that with security gates. People scared for a break-in, they don't want to wait.

NAMHLA: That's Mr Combrink? The gentleman through there? [*She indicates the workshop.*]

SHANELL: Ja, he's the … [*hugely apologetic*] Ag, sorry, man! Where's my blimmen manners? My husband's Dwayne Combrink ('brink' as in 'think'). Me, I'm his wife. I'm Shanell. With a 'S'.

NAMHLA: Namhla Gumede.

SHANELL: Nam …?

NAMHLA: Namhla.

SHANELL: Namhla. Nice. [*Beat.*] Is that now your normal name?

NAMHLA [*distracted*]: I'm sorry?

SHANELL: No, it's just … [*she bumbles on again*] … Jonas had a normal name and a tribal name. His tribal name was like Themba-Themba-something, but he never used it because white people, he said, they always messed it up. [*Beat.*] Not that people don't mess up my name, hey. It's what happens when you take two names and stick them together. [*She responds to a curious look from her guest.*] No, you see, we English. My gran on my mom's side was Sharlene and my ouma on my dad's was Ronelle. They stuck the two combined and … ja, well. [*Beat.*] Wasn't so funny growing up, I tell you! Chantal … Chardonell. Some kids they even called me Chanel Number 5. [*She snorts.*]. Alla' time I was Child Number 4!

NAMHLA [*not wildly into this*]: Will he be long, your husband?

22

Beat.

SHANELL [*'light bulb'*]: Aaah, wait-a-minute! [*She is hugely relieved.*] Here am I thinking it's metalwork you want, meantime it's collecting!

NAMHLA has no idea what she means.

SHANELL: Somebody owes you, they disappear off the planet you come to the Debt Collector. Oh, my goodness! [*She plays the hostess.*] Okay. Orraight. Um … can I offer you some tea, some coffee? [NAMHLA *looks at her without responding.*] No?

NAMHLA: Thank you, no.

SHANELL: Always catches me out. People, they come in here you can see it on their faces. Shame. It's not so much actually embarrassed, as like, Ooo, hel, how am I now gonna ask this person to … you know? They been to lawyers, attorneys, even the bally cops can't sort them out. What do they do? They go to the Man that Can! [*She tosses detritus from the seating areas.*] Siddown, siddown … or wait … [*indicating.*] You wanna rather go sit in the lounge? This place is like … no? OK. [*She pats the car seat.*] Sit, sit. [NAMHLA *complies.*] No, you know … starts off all friendly and if you lucky it's over in two ticks. They don't play along, out he goes with this blimmen baseball bat, his gun, and I'm thinking, Ooo, gonna, is he ever coming back? But he always does. [*Proclaiming.*] Dependable Dwayne makes those cash worries verdwyn! He's a pain in the backside sometimes, but, ja, that's another story. [*She needs a drink.*] Listen, are you sure you don't want just a tiny glass of …

NAMHLA: I'm fine, thank you.

SHANELL: You won't mind if I …?

NAMHLA: Not at all.

> *SHANELL moves to the box wine on top of the fridge and pours herself a drink.*

SHANELL: He won't be long. [*She moves to the entrance of the workshop, a big hint.*] He's gotta take a break sooner or later, and then … [*The sound of an angle-grinder, sparks and all, forces her to give up on this approach.*] Ja, it's hard for everybody right now, hey … we all farming backwards. And living out here on the bladdy plots … sjoe! Not for nothing we called Far East Gate & Fence. [*She snorts and returns with a drink.*] And that's another bowl of contention. Half the people who phone in here think we Chinese. You pick up the phone, first thing they ask – Can you speak English? Hell. I've begged him I dunno how many times to change it. No, he says, we live on the Far East Rand, we Far East Gate & Fence. [*She tries again.*] You sure I can't get you … [*taps her glass*]?

NAMHLA: I'm good, thank you.

> *There is an awkward pause. SHANELL has finally run out of steam.*

SHANELL: So now you, hey … where you from? You not from, like, Springs?

NAMHLA: My home is in Duxberry.

SHANELL [*clueless*]: Ducks …

NAMHLA: Morningside … Johannesburg.

SHANELL: Ah … [*little laugh.*] Nice. [*She settles down beside her guest on the car seat.*] Ja, you know it's interesting they now calling this place Ekurhuleni, hey. Don't have to wonder anymore if we living in Brakpan, Boksburg or the Dark-Side-of-the-blimmen-Moon.

NAMHLA [*deadpan*]: Joburg's not exactly Earth Central.

SHANELL: Better than stuck out here. [*She snorts.*] You know what me and my friends we call this place, hey? The Bra-Bok-Noni Triangle. 'Cos just like the one in Bermuda everything that goes into it sommer disappears. [*Conspiratorial.*] You know, I hear there's a family coupla' kays down the road here … they knock themselves out with sleeping pills every night. They could trash the house, carry them off in their very own beds, nobody be none the wiser.

NAMHLA [*unconvinced*]: That sounds like an urban legend.

SHANELL: Maybe so, but I tell you right now … living out here is Not Lekker. [*Warily.*] Don't tell him that, hey … [*She jerks her head towards the workshop.*] He thinks this is like the best place on God's Green Earth.

Beat.

NAMHLA: How long have you lived here?

SHANELL [*mortified, unable to comprehend it*]: Too long. Nearly twenty years … Dwayne's been here like forever.

NAMHLA: And he was married before?

SHANELL: Before?

NAMHLA: Before you, I mean. Was he … divorced, or …

SHANELL: No, please. The Cradle Snatcher left it late. He was forty orreddy when him and me we tied the knot. I thought, ja, okay, we live here on the plots a few

25

years, build up a bit of a nest egg, go live in, like – I dunno – Little Falls, Ruimsig. Maybe move down to the coast somewhere. [*She snorts disdainfully.*] No, it was all going so nice, you know, first few years … and then Dwayne decides to go into partnership with this real bladdy chancer. The sly windgat goes out and buys all these motor vehicles, smart-fancy equipment and then sommer ups and disappears. Dwayne's still in the dwang and Flash Harry Serfontein is sitting in Toronto, San Diego … somebody said last year they saw him in Bali! Bali! This world is really, like … I dunno.

NAMHLA: Things seldom pan out the way we'd like them to.

SHANELL: My life in a nutshell. [*Reflective.*] It's all so different, you know, when you like still young and thinking, ja, okay … what now? I mean, there I was, hey … First Princess, Miss Foschini Pageant in Krugersdorp. I'm going out with this guy who's now swotting to be a … ag, what do they call them again?

DWAYNE drifts in from the workshop in time to catch this hoary old chestnut. He wipes his hands on a greasy cloth and moves behind the car seat.

DWAYNE: Well, well, well … if it isn't the Chartered bladdy Accountant story. [*Beat.*] Stranger walks into the house … five minutes she's trotting out the tale of The-One-That-Got-Away. [*SHANELL has not flinched.*] Why not just sommer cut to the chase, baby shoes? [*He 'performs' to impress their guest.*] Lourens Mynhardt, retired corporate executive, now living on the Sunshine Coast and Commander-in-Chief of all the Bells and Whistles.

SHANELL [*not missing a beat*]: Well put, my darling.

DWAYNE: All she gets from Yours Truly is Deci-bells and
Dust … Uphill. One towering mishoop after another.

SHANELL [*smiling sweetly*]: I'm so lucky my better-half's
got such a thick skin.

DWAYNE: Grows thicker by the day.

SHANELL: Pretty soon it'll be as thick as that of a rhino.

Pow! Right between the eyes. A beat, before DWAYNE
snipes back.

DWAYNE: You can't organise a drink for our guest?

NAMHLA: I'm good. Really, I'm …

SHANELL: You be pleased to know our visitor has a job for
you. Mrs Gamede …

NAMHLA: Gumede.

SHANELL: Mrs Gumede's got somebody that owes her.

DWAYNE: Is that right?

SHANELL [*cuttingly*]: Real bum-in-the-butter time for you,
hey? Chance to go out, bash a few heads, and get paid
for the privilege. [*She gives her husband a withering
look.*] Some of us should be so lucky!

DWAYNE: Wanna have a shot at it, feel free.

SHANELL: No, no. I've got far more exciting things to do …
like sweet-talking the municipality into not cutting
our water and lights. [*She turns to their guest.*] So nice
to meet you, Mrs Gumede. [*She heads across to her
purchases.*] Don't let him hit you too hard with the
commission. Sees a car like yours outside, his fee goes
straight through the roof.

SHANELL leaves, carting off her precious merchandise.

27

DWAYNE watches her go.

DWAYNE [*chuckling mirthlessly*]: I must apologise for my wife. Once she gets started it's like a burst sewerage pipe on Main Street.

He turns his back on the visitor, scratching around on his desk for a pen and paper. NAMHLA slips her hand into her handbag and draws out a small firearm.

DWAYNE: Right. First things first. I don't do Revenge. I don't do Pay Back. I Collect, pure and simple. You tell me who it is that owes you, where I can find them and the total amount outstanding.

As he turns to her she slips the gun back in her bag.

NAMHLA [*unflustered*]: That's it?
DWAYNE: That, and then the little question a' commission.

Beat.

NAMHLA [*ice cold*]: And the man I'm looking for … he'll pay his debt in full?
DWAYNE [*chuckling*]: All I can promise is my best shot.

The phone on the desk rings. DWAYNE is in full-on flirting mode.

DWAYNE: If that's who I think it is, we'll have to put this on hold. [*He whips up the phone.*] Ja? Mrs de Freitas … ja, ja, I'm sorry … ja, I know. What you need's a dog. When it comes to security dog's your first line a' defence. [*He beams.*] Not funny, ja, I know. [*He nods.*] First thing tomorrow, you have my word. [*He ends the call and says, bitterly*] This woman's beginning to grate me something chronic.

While DWAYNE *is on the phone* NAMIILA *opens her handbag again and digs around.*

NAMHLA: I'd like to make an appointment as soon as possible.

DWAYNE: No problem.

NAMHLA [*handing him her business card*]: My number. Call me any time.

DWAYNE [*trying to be cute*]: Whoo-aah! Not often I score a lady's number this fast, hey? [*Reading.*] Namhla … [*Brightly*] Namhlanje. That's 'today'.

NAMHLA [*deadpan*]: The man speaks isiZulu.

DWAYNE: The man doesn't even come close.

NAMHLA: Perhaps today's the day the journey begins.

He chortles and she appears emotionless. Again they speak simultaneously.

NAMHLA: ''Til next time.

DWAYNE: 'Til next time.

They stare at each other. He is clearly hitting on her.

DWAYNE: We gotta stop doing this.

The choral voices of Simunye (KwaZulu Senzeni) bleed in … growing louder … louder still … as the lights slowly fade to scene-change mode.

Scene 3

Night. Several days later.

Lights fade up as the music slowly fades out.

SHANELL is at the window, clutching a wine glass, peering out through the blinds. She is dressed-to-impress, heavily made up. A bottle of white wine, less than half of it left, stands on the desk. Although not yet intoxicated SHANELL is ticking rather nicely and is involved in an animated conversation on her smart phone.

SHANELL [*into the phone, pleading*]: No! No! That's not how it is and you know it! If I could be there now I'd be there! Don't do this to me, my angel, please! It's not fair! You not the only one who has to make sacrifices. [*She frowns.*] And listen, I dunno about that wedding, hey. It's hard for me to get away on a weekend! [*With feeling.*] I don't care if there's lotsa' strangers around. You-me, we dancing, next thing we all over Facebook. [*She drifts away from the window.*] I'm not being difficult, my babes. You forgotten orready that last time at the Spur, the Lakeside Mall. Candice wanted to take that selfie with you, me and her in front of the Big Wheel. [*She is adamant.*] No, no! God alone knows what he'd do if he ever found out! And anyway, who organises a wedding in a blimmen lapa for heavensake? A lapa in a game park that isn't even a game park! [*She rolls her eyes.*] Ah, please, man! It's five kays other side a' Brakpan! A stupid little safari

lodge with a couple of warthogs, a moth-eaten zebra
and a giraffe that looks like it's about drop down dead
any minute! [*She tries to smooth things over.*] I'm not
tryna' make excuses now, my angel, I'm just ... Where
am I? I've just told you, man, I'm still at home! I'm
waiting for him to get back. [*She moves back to the
window.*] Ag, he's got this blimmen woman coming,
wants him to ... [*She gets tearful.*] Don't say things
like that, my baba, this is bladdy hard for me too,
dammit! [*Desperate.*] I'll be there, I'll be there ... just
give me like twenny minutes, half an hour. Oo, hell!

*From off stage comes the sound of a powerful, top-of-
the-range motor car approaching and the strobe effect
of headlights through the blinds causes* SHANELL *to dart
to the window again. The vehicle engine is switched off.*

SHANELL [*into phone*]: It's him! I have to go! I'll see you
now-now ... ja, ja. [*She peers through the blinds.*] Oh,
shit, it's her! I still gotta go. [*She giggles.*] Sis, man,
don't be rude ... ja, ja ... later ... stop it! [*Turned on
by something he has just suggested, she is breathless.*] Ja
... ja ... love you, too.

*She clicks off her phone and heads for the front door,
cursing under her breath.*

SHANELL [*off*]: Mrs Gumede. Hi. Good evening.
NAMHLA [*off*]: Hello.
SHANELL [*off*]: Come in, come in. Watch your step.

SHANELL *follows a mildly flustered* NAMHLA *in. The
visitor again wears an elegant, stylish outfit that is in
stark contrast to the flashy apparel worn by her hostess.*

NAMHLA: The traffic on the highway's impossible.

SHANELL: Don't stress. Dwayne's actually not back yet. It's pathetic! [*She speed dials on her phone.*] He's collected for Stavros before. [*She holds the phone to her ear, making no effort to conceal her frustration.*] But then again, the kind of gangsters that owe Themi blimmen Stavros, less said about them, the better.

A beat, before a muffled cellphone ring to the tune of the William Tell Overture is heard coming from the direction of the trash heap of a desk.

SHANELL [*anger building, muttering*]: Urgh! Why am I not surprised!

Highly irritated, SHANELL scratches around on the desk, eventually finding an old, grubby cellphone ringing away. She cuts her call and the ringing stops.

SHANELL: Lies around on this stupid blimmen desk alla' time gathering dust! [*At the end of her tether, she tosses it down angrily.*]

NAMHLA: Never mind. [*She perches on the car seat.*]

SHANELL: No, I do mind. It's beyond a joke! I mean, you should see him tryna' operate the thing … takes him half-a-bladdy hour to tap out a three-line SMS. Try teach him predictive text he goes into anabolic shock.

NAMHLA [*unable to stop herself*]: Anaphylactic.

SHANELL: Ana-flippen-whatever! Playing the dumb-stupid doff-bag just to spite me … shit! [*She mutters angrily.*] So much for loving the life you live. [*Quick-fire, brightly.*] You love the life you live, Mrs Gumede?

NAMHLA [*one step behind*]: You mean, do I …?

32

SHANELL: Can't love the life you live if you not living the life you love, hey?

NAMHLA is clearly thinking 'How-do-I-respond-to-this?'

SHANELL crosses to the front door, anxiously checking her watch.

NAMHLA [*warily*]: Forgive me, I'm not … interrupting anything?

SHANELL [*irate*]: No, no … there's this friend of mine, she's going through this whole … domestic-marital … urgh! Should just sommer walk out the door!

NAMHLA [*indicating*]: If you'd rather I waited outside in my …

SHANELL: No, please! [*Fuming.*] He drives me stark-raving mad! [*Appealing to the heavens.*] I try, Em … every day, I try! I promise!

SHANELL becomes aware that what she is doing might appear a bit weird. NAMHLA watches, mesmerised. SHANELL gives a sheepish little giggle.

SHANELL: Ag, don't mind me. [*She crosses to the car seat.*] I was a kid my mother had this old school friend. Always coming up with these, you know … breathe deep … find your centre, stuff-like-that. [*Emphatic.*] Rule Number One: most important thing in the world – love the life you live, and live the life you love.

NAMHLA: Ah.

SHANELL: Lord alone knows what she'd say she saw me today! [*Beat.*] Emily Cathcart. She was an air hostess for Pan American Airways.

NAMHLA: Living that kind of life the loving must have come easy.

SHANELL: Oh, she loved it alright. Always immaculate … nails … make-up … full toetie. She wore this … pencil-slim uniform, tiny hat tilted to one side … little wings. [*A fond recollection.*] She had this walk … they taught them to walk in those days … down the aisle, you know, on the aeroplane … up and down. [*Smiling.*] She used to show me how, and I'd be like … tummy in, chin up.

SHANELL goes into a gentle, hip-swaying walk.

SHANELL: It was kind of, like … captivating, she called it. Sexy, but not too sexy … sort of like …

NAMHLA: Alluring.

SHANELL: Al … that, ja … but also, like, you know …

NAMHLA: Discreet.

SHANELL: There's it. [*She perches on the swivel chair, picking up her wine glass.*] Flight attendant. That was gonna be me one day. [*Wistfully.*] The places she went, the people she met … [*Breathily.*] Ladies and gentlemen … [*She places her empty wine glass just below her mouth to create a perfect tannoy sound.*] Ladies and gentlemen, your attention, please. At this time we request that all passengers return to their seats … and then my best … We will shortly be landing in Honolulu. Honolulu. It was the most gorgeous-beautiful name I'd ever heard in my whole life. [*Beat, snapping out of it.*] Just listen to me. [*She indicates the wine bottle on the desk.*] Can I offer you some Stein? It's dry-white.

NAMHLA [*ponders*]: Since we both seem to be waiting for …
SHANELL: Fantastic. Drinking alone's the bally pits!

[*Crossing to the desk she picks up the wine bottle, only to discover that her husband's 'Barber of Seville' sketch is stuck to the bottom. She squirms as she detaches it.*] Serves him right for having such a horrible messy desk.

She gives the sketch a quick wipe before handing it to her guest.

NAMHLA [*reading*]: 'Barber of Seville'.
SHANELL: Spanish. Mrs de Freitas. She's Portuguese.
NAMHLA: Quite some design.

SHANELL has picked up her husband's grubby brandy glass from the desk. She speaks while she crosses to the basin to rinse the glass out with tap water.

SHANELL: Ja, well. [*Grimly.*] If she hadn't insisted on all the twiddles and twirls she wouldn't have had to come in here screaming blue murder 'cos it wasn't ready on time.

She returns to the desk, shaking excess water from the glass. As she pours wine into the 'clean' brandy glass for NAMHLA, *her smart phone rings. She picks it up and checks the screen.*

NAMHLA: Your husband?
SHANELL [*flustered*]: No, no, it's my … um … [*Phone to her ear.*] Hello! Hello! [*To* NAMHLA] The signal's very bad in here. [*Into phone.*] Sorry, the signal's very bad here!

She heads off through the alcove.

NAMHLA places the sketch on the desk and moves across to the basin to pour most of the wine down the drain. She walks over to the window, peering out into the night.

SHANELL returns, completing her call as she enters.

SHANELL [*into the phone*]: Okay … see you at the Dros. [*She snaps off the phone, relieved.*] Okay, everything's sorted. Everybody knows what's what.

NAMHLA moves away from the window, a look of concern on her face.

NAMHLA: You don't ever feel vulnerable out here?

SHANELL: Ag, when Dwayne's around it's fine. On the nights he was out doing his thing there was always ol' Jonas. [*Reflective.*] I think he kind of liked that … making sure the madam was safe. Shame. [*She strokes the blanket on the backrest of the car seat.*] Still can't believe we'll never see him again.

Beat.

NAMHLA: How did he …? Was he ill, or …?

SHANELL: Ag, too terrible, man. He was coming in from Sebokeng on the Friday morning. [*Bitterly.*] At the plaza there by Vosloorus where he changes taxis there's this whole gemors … drivers shouting and screaming … gaaning aan. Next thing they pulling out pangas and guns … there's bullets flying everywhere. One a' the drivers jumps in his taxi and pulls off at like a hundred kays an hour. They say when he hit Jonas he slammed his head into the wall like one a' those shop-dummy things.

NAMHLA: Oh, my oath.

SHANELL: They said he was dead before the paramedics even arrived. [*Beat.*] That was almost six weeks ago. Dwayne's been like … destroyed. They met when they were both teenagers. [*She shakes her head.*] They'd kill for each other, those two. I once saw Dwayne smash a oke half to death just for calling him the k-word. [*Beat.*] The mornings I'd come in here, find ol' Jonas fast asleep on this car seat. On the nights they worked late, the two of them, crooning away in this workshop. There were times I'm thinking I hear *Blueberry Hill* just once more, strue's God, I'm gonna throw myself under a bus.

NAMLA: That was Fats Domino.

SHANELL: Sorry?

NAMHLA: I know that song.

SHANELL: All I know it was their stuck-record-forever blimmen theme song.

Beat.

NAMHLA: Must be hard.

SHANELL: For Dwayne, ja, 'specially. But as they say, hey … Such is life.

Beat.

NAMHLA: It's always fascinated me the way a particular song never leaves you.

SHANELL [*gleefully*]: Boney M!

NAMHLA [*rolling her eyes*]: Urgh!

SHANELL: What? You don't like them?

NAMHLA: I'm sorry. I hear Boney M and I'm crawling up the wall. [*She shudders.*] Give me nails on a chalkboard any day.

SHANELL: Boney M for me, and it's Christmas time. [*Wistfully.*] Kids laughing, gaaning-aan … splashing about on the slip-'n-slide morning 'til night.

NAMHLA: These are your children?

SHANELL: My children? [*She's thrown.*] No. No. No such luck. [*She gulps at her wine.*]

NAMHLA [*mortified*]: I'm … I'm so sorry.

SHANELL: No, it's fine.

NAMHLA: I didn't mean to …

SHANELL: Ag, please. [*Downbeat.*] It's not that I never wanted kids. It's just … ja. Things are what they are. For Dwayne it was different. He's always been like … ja, well, hashtag, just saying. [*Beat.*] We had all the tests … the whole … rigmarole. Everything was fine. No problems, both of us … down there, I mean. [*She indicates her genital organs.*] But, like they say, you know, it's not always about what's down there, it's about what's up here. [*She taps her temple.*] And with Dwayne, he …

NAMHLA: He, what?

SHANELL [*miles away*]: Ag, I just wonder sometimes … men … always looking for a back door. [*She snorts, snapping out of it.*] All he can do is make jokes about it … about what a hoot it is for a man who carries a gun to have to admit he shoots blanks. [*She spits out angrily.*] I hate it when he does that! You have any kids?

NAMHLA [*flustered*]: Me? I … cr … so far … not yet. My husband is, um … we've only been married a couple of years, and with all his commitments …

SHANELL: He's, like, round-the-clock?

NAMHLA: He's a … fixer … middle-man. Administers all these major international transactions. His long-term ambitions, though, lie in politics.

SHANELL: Wow!

NAMHLA: Lanford Gumede. You may have heard of him.

SHANELL: Er … [*She hasn't.*]

NAMHLA: Spends ninety percent of his time outside of the country … meetings, negotiations, engagements that require him to be away months on end.

SHANELL: Sjoe!

NAMHLA: Even when he's at home there are people, in and out, all the time … bodyguards, politicos … what do they call them these days … *tenderpreneurs.*

SHANELL: If I said ships-in-the-night …

NAMHLA [*mirthless chuckle*]: Ours is more a case of two tiny ships in a great big ocean on a night as dark as Hades.

SHANELL: Not so good for making babies.

NAMHLA: I'd settle for a ten-minute conversation, face-to-face. [*Reflective.*] I look at him tearing around in fast forward all the time and I sometimes wonder … is it really ambition, or just quiet desperation? [*SHANELL doesn't have a clue what she means.*]
Most men lead lives of quiet desperation … and go to the grave with the song still in them. Henry Thoreau … 19th-century philosopher.

SHANELL [*out of her depth*]: Yes. So for you by the house, it
must be, like …

NAMHLA: Oh, fear not. I keep myself busy.

SHANELL: Ja?

NAMHLA: Writing articles … submitting material …

SHANELL: You a writer?

NAMHLA: By the time I got to O-levels I already knew that
the written word was my calling card … features …
reportage … communication. The big dream for me
was one day running my very own magazine.

SHANELL: Oprah, eat your heart out.

NAMHLA [*ironic chuckle*]: You leave the hallowed halls
of academia clutching your precious degree, and
whoop-de-doo, the world awaits! Pretty soon you
find yourself out there tilting at windmills like all the
other would-be scribes. [*She gives a wry, never-say-die
chuckle.*] There's always a novel, though … somewhere
… lurking.

SHANELL: A book?

NAMHLA: Maybe two. Please God, a whole string of them.

SHANELL: Ja, like that … Rowling … Whats-her-name?
Harry Potter woman. Or this new lady now … all that
sex-porno-handcuffy stuff.

NAMHLA: E L James.

SHANELL: My husband calls it *Fifty Shades of Kak*! I made
half the money that woman makes he be kissing my
feet.

NAMHLA: Never too late.

SHANELL: For you maybe. Me, I get a headache writing out
a bally shopping list.

NAMHLA: Don't we all?

Beat.

SHANELL: No, you know, when you first came in here the
other day, I heard you talk, I said to myself, ja … this
lady's definitely not, like … local.

NAMHLA: Local? [*The penny drops.*] Oh, you mean from
here? No, I'm not. Although I was, originally. Unlike
my husband I've spent a good part of my life in that
artificial, sanitised bubble they call Exile.

SHANELL: Overseas.

NAMLA: Wasn't through choice I might add. [*Mock
serious.*] We're talking the Dark Old Days. [*Seeing
SHANELL's clueless look.*] BD!

SHANELL [*still lost*]: Yes?

NAMHLA: Before Democracy.

SHANELL: Oh, ja. [*Beat.*] Freedom's here, but there's still
problems, hey.

NAMHLA [*bitter, half to herself*]: Wheeling and dealing and
grab what you can.

*Pause … SHANELL pours more wine and pops the
question she's been dying to ask.*

SHANELL: So. Who is it that … actually … owes you?

NAMHLA [*preoccupied*]: I beg your pardon?

SHANELL: I was just wondering who it is you want my
husband to look for?

NAMHLA [*showing a side of her we haven't yet seen*]: I
would've thought that's a private matter between your
husband and myself.

SHANELL: Oh. Ja. Sorry. [*She is flustered.*] It's just …

41

Dwayne's not the only debt collector around and I was wondering how you … [*She breaks off, irritated.*] Dammit! Where is he now, man? This is getting blimmen ridiculous!

She heads for the window, peeking through the blinds and squinting into the night.

NAMHLA [*subtly probing again*]: The other day you told me your husband's lived in this place 'forever'. When you say forever …

SHANELL: No, it just seems to me like forever. He came here long before I showed up. This house was even more in the sticks in those days … wasn't a building for miles around. He fixed the place up … started with his welding. One thing led to another, and …

NAMHLA: And that was forty-odd years ago?

SHANELL: About, ja. [*She looks at her guest and grins.*]: Sjoe! So this is how you do it, hey?

NAMHLA [*thrown*]: I'm sorry?

SHANELL [*impishly*]: This is how it works with writers when you looking for … what-d'you-callit? … fishing for juicy stuff. [*She responds to* NAMHLA*'s wry smile.*] No, it's okay. I don't mind. It's just … hell's teeth, talk about dull and boring! Highlight of the week for us is counting the ducks down by the dam on a Sunday afternoon.

NAMHLA [*speaking from experience*]: There's no such thing as a dull or boring life. A hard life, maybe … a sad or tragic life …

SHANELL: Ja, 'cos that can osso change, hey. [*She blurts out.*] Like now, with me and Dwayne. Something amazing's come up; we can hardly believe our luck!

NAMHLA [*deadpan*]: How very nice for you.

SHANELL: Ja, it's … [*Stops, suddenly terrified she's blown it.*]
Ag, that's how life goes, you know … up and down.
What do they say? Merry-go-rounds and …

NAMHLA: Swings and roundabouts.

SHANELL: Ja, ja. [*Flustered, deflecting.*] And to think it was
just luck I met him in the first place, hey. It's true.
If I hadn't gone to Vivien Ferreira's baby shower in
Benoni that time, I wouldn't even be here today. [*She's
babbling now.*] I was still living on the West Rand
and this friend of mine was having her first child. I'm
coming down Tom Jones in my Beetle, I'm orreedy
late and would you believe it – gwa-dah – pothole like
two feet deep! I'm thinking, 'Ooo, lekker, now what?'
[*Checking an imaginary rear-view mirror, thrilled.*]
And there he is … pulling up behind me – my knight
on a shining white … bakkie.

Beat.

NAMHLA [*rueful chuckle*]: My shining knight was bare-
chested.

SHANELL [*startled*]: Bare what? Who was this?

NAMHLA: When I first met Lanford he was wearing
ibheshu. [SHANELL *has no idea what she's talking
about.*] Urgh! Made such a fool of myself.

SHANELL [*hugely intrigued*]: Tell me.

NAMHLA: No, I can't, I …

SHANELL: No, come on, man! Tell me!

Beat.

NAMHLA: I was a guest at this traditional wedding

ceremony down in KZN. You have to remember, here's a woman who's spent the bulk of her childhood in England where weddings are civilised, refined and oh-so-la-di-da. [*Mortified, she is unable to proceed.*] Uuuugh!

SHANELL: What? What?

NAMHLA: I should have realised the moment I saw the ox.

SHANELL: Ox?

NAMHLA: Huge ox being led out.

SHANELL: Don't tell me!

NAMHLA: It was the instant I saw that assegai plunging into its neck my legs went from under me.

SHANELL: No!

NAMHLA: Gone! Out like a light.

SHANELL: You didn't need to come from England for that to happen. I'da been flat out on the floor with you.

NAMHLA: When I came around, there he was … Lanford Gumede … most eligible bachelor at the gathering, sweeping me off to more genteel surroundings.

SHANELL [*awestruck*]: That is so romantic.

NAMHLA [*not so sure*]: Hmm.

SHANELL: And now here you are. Hitched, and living in the RSA.

NAMHLA: I can't help wondering what my life would be like if I'd stayed on in England. Still single, perhaps … carefree … no 'significant other' to consider.

A distracted SHANELL *heads for the window, peering out through the blinds.*

SHANELL: Hell, I hope it's not one of those blimmen dead-end streets. He hangs around forever, meantime they given him the slip. Or he's chasing some gom-gat and the oke's climbed up a tree! It's happened before, you know.

NAMHLA: Where's the pay off?

SHANELL: Huh?

NAMHLA: There's his commission, I see that, but what about the risks?

SHANELL: Ag, that doesn't worry Dwayne. He skriks for niks. Never mind where angels fear to go, Satan himself won't go where Dwayne goes. You looking at a person who killed a man before he was twelve years old. [*She stops, mortified.*] Sorry! I've had too much to drink.

NAMHLA: He killed a man?

Beat.

SHANELL [*flustered*]: He didn't actually … it wasn't, like … murder or anything?

NAMHLA [*quietly*]: You can kill a person without murdering them?

SHANELL [*looking about, terrified the walls might have ears*]: If he knew I was telling you this, he'd … [*Hoping to be let off the hook.*] It was a black man. He didn't mean it … it was … kind of like an accident.

NAMHLA [*gently*]: Accidents happen.

SHANELL [*taking a deep breath, knowing there is no going back*]: When Dwayne was still a kid they lived in this little town the other side of Delmas. His father got his kicks riding around on the weekends using road signs for target practice.

NAMHLA: You mean he shot at them?

SHANELL [*hesitating, before ploughing on*]: Dwayne said he

hated it because his father forced him to go with him and he'd always drive with a bottle of brandy stuck between his legs. [*Beat.*] The more dronk the oke got, the more he'd shout and laugh … cackling away like this was supposed to be like one moersa big jol. [*She looks about.*] This one day they driving along, he suddenly gives the gun to Dwayne. He tells him he must now have a go … he must shoot. Now Dwayne is still a laaitie, hey, he's never even hardly held a gun, never mind shot at a road sign going full-speed. [*Beat.*] Dwayne says 'no'. His father gives him a stiff klap, straight in the mouth. Says 'what's his problem' – 'you a girl now, or what?' So, coming up ahead is this road sign. It says 'Ogies, 5 miles'. Dwayne's father says, 'OK – the 'O' in Ogies – aim for that'. Dwayne doesn't know what he's doing, hey, he sommer shoots … [*She's come to the 'heavy' part.*] But now, as they go past the sign Dwayne thinks he sees something in the grass … the long grass in the veld behind the sign … a flash, a white flash, like a shirt, maybe! He screams to his father, 'Stop! Go back!' He wants to take a look … see what he's done.

NAMHLA: His father goes back?

SHANELL: Where from? His father says 'what you tjanking about now? So you killed one of them, so what? One less to worry about'. [*Beat. NAMHLA is horrified.*] They get home, his father's so vrot he crashes out in the lounge, falls asleep. Dwayne grabs his bike … he rides to that place as fast as he can. But now it's getting dark … it's not so easy anymore, you know, to see. He gets to the road-sign ... there in the veld behind it he finds this open can of pilchards ... half-eaten loaf of bread ... and blood on the grass! He looks, and he looks, all over ... nothing! But now he doesn't sommer los it, hey, he rides back to town, to the hospital. Hell. Here's this eleven-and-a-half-year-old kid in the Non-European section looking for a black man in a white shirt. 'Hey, laaitie ... what you doing here? Voetsek!' They kick him out, don't wanna know his story. [*Beat.*] Shame. He tried so hard.

NAMHLA: Did they ever ... was the body ever found?

SHANELL: Not that he knew. Dwayne went looking in the Bantu location for days after that ... wandering around those dusty streets no white man would ever go. I can sorta' picture it, you know ... snotty-nose kid ... can't stop crying ... looking for something he doesn't know what.

A beat ... the sound of a high-powered bakkie approaching, pulling up on the gravel outside. Headlights through the blinds snap off. The engine is killed.

SHANELL [*relieved*]: Jeez! At last!

NAMHLA: Is that him?

SHANELL looks out through the window before turning back to NAMHLA.

SHANELL [*frantic*]: Listen, please don't breathe a word about ...

NAMHLA: Of course.

SHANELL: Because he told me that story a long time ago, and ...

NAMHLA: Absolutely.

SHANELL [*grabbing her keys and handbag*]: And don't make him do anything too dangerous. In his head he thinks he's blimmen Iron Man, but one of these days, s'trues God, he's gonna bite off more than can chew. [*She leaves.*] OK, bye!

No sooner has SHANELL *disappeared than she lets out a scream.*

DWAYNE [*off*]: Aaargh! Bugger-it!

DWAYNE lurches in, holding a soggy lump of toilet paper beneath his left hand. Blood pours from a savage wound across his palm. SHANELL follows him.

SHANELL: Oh, for heavensake! [*Furious.*] Like I need this right now!

DWAYNE [*seething*]: Doos took the gap. The septic fuck!

SHANELL: Watch the blood on the floor, man!

DWAYNE notices their stunned guest and is concerned about having made her wait.

DWAYNE: Mrs Gumede, my apologies.

NAMHLA: Not at all. [*She opens her handbag.*] Here, let me …

She takes a handkerchief from her handbag, tries to staunch the bleeding.

DWAYNE [*crying out in pain*]: Sssssss, eina!

SHANELL: Let's get you to the clinic.

She shoves him towards the alcove.

DWAYNE: It's nothing. Los it.

He pulls away to head for the washbasin.

SHANELL: What d'you mean it's nothing? Look at this! [*She indicates the floor.*]

DWAYNE: What really pisses me off is that the fucking bird has flown! [*To their guest.*] 'Scuse my language. [*He turns on the tap.*] Stavros is gonna love this.

SHANELL: Stavros can go collect himself! [*She pulls at him.*] Come to the bathroom!

DWAYNE [*to NAMHLA, as he is yanked off*]: Sorry about this, man.

NAMHLA crosses to turn off the tap. She then moves to the desk and opens a drawer, scratching about. She locates a bunch of keys and tries to unlock the new padlock on Jonas's old locker. The sudden ringing of her smart phone startles her. She removes the phone from her handbag and looks at the screen before taking the call.

NAMHLA [*into the phone, emotionless*]: Yes … [*She frowns.*] Sorry, say that again. Singapore? Ah, Beijing. [*She listens, dead calm.*] No, Lanford, no. Get one of your minions to take you to the air … What do you mean? I'm busy with my research, you know that. My work is also import … [*She nods, grimly.*] Fine, fine … okay. I'll think about it … yes … yes … fine … yes … g'night … you too.

She snaps off her phone, staring blankly at the screen. Plopping the phone back into her handbag, she tries with a different key to unlock the padlock.

DWAYNE enters through the alcove, his wounded hand wrapped in a makeshift face-cloth bandage. NAMHLA quickly ducks into the workshop.

DWAYNE [*speaking as he enters*]: OK, let's get moving on this thing.

He looks up to discover his office is empty and crosses to the window to look out. NAMHLA emerges from the workshop and pops the bunch of keys back into the desk drawer, closing it, before DWAYNE turns around.

DWAYNE [*spotting her*]: I thought you decided to split.

SHANELL comes in, irritated. She carries the blood-soaked hanky belonging to their visitor.

SHANELL [*angry*]: Dwayne! Your hand needs stitches!
DWAYNE: Bull, man! Got a meeting here.

SHANELL holds the hanky up and waves it about.

SHANELL: We'll need to get you another one.
NAMHLA: Don't worry about it.

SHANELL drops the hanky into the waste bin and notices her bloodied hands. No sooner has she disappeared through the alcove to wash her hands than a muttering DWAYNE heads across to pour himself a stiff double brandy.

DWAYNE: Murphy's bladdy Law, man … everything that can go wrong implodes!

While DWAYNE's back is turned NAMHLA reaches into the waste bin and retrieves the hanky. Spotting a take-

away box on the floor, she picks it up, depositing the hanky in it and slipping it into her handbag.

DWAYNE heads for his desk, drink in hand, searching for a pen and notebook.

DWAYNE: Right. Let's get some details here.

NAMHLA: I think we ought to leave it for now.

DWAYNE: Sorry?

NAMHLA: I need to go home and you need to get that hand sorted.

DWAYNE: But …

NAMHLA: I've just been informed I have to be up at 4.30.

Beat.

DWAYNE: Hell, man. [*He studies his hand.*] This is embarrassing.

NAMHLA fixes him with a determined, no-nonsense look.

NAMHLA: Let's reschedule. We need to meet privately.

DWAYNE misinterprets her mood, believing she is hitting on him. SHANELL returns with a couple of pain killers.

SHANELL [*to DWAYNE*]: Here. Take these.

He knocks them back with a slug of brandy.

NAMHLA: Right. I'll be on my way.

SHANELL: You're going? Aren't you, like … [*She indicates her husband.*]

DWAYNE [*smiling at their guest*]: Mrs Gumede reckons I can't cut it.

NAMHLA: I'll call you in the morning.

DWAYNE: No, sweet.

NAMHLA: And get that hand seen to. I need you to be on top of your game.

SHANELL [*heading out, texting*]: Listen, I'm sorry about this mess, hey.

NAMHLA [*turning to DWAYNE*]: Goodnight.

SHANELL [*focused fully now on her phone*]: Okay, bye.

NAMHLA leaves.

Still trying to process what has just happened, DWAYNE moves around to the front of the desk, his pulse racing. SHANELL finishes texting.

From offstage comes the sound of the top-of-the-range car starting up … a change of gears and the vehicle pulls away, the sound fading into the distance.

SHANELL [*hyped up and about to leave*]: So? How did it go?

DWAYNE: Knew something wasn't right moment I pulled in.

SHANELL [*cuttingly*]: I'm not talking about the job. I'm talking about the Sale! [*Beat.*] You said you were going to see him today. This Vietnamese.

DWAYNE [*subdued*]: Mr Li.

SHANELL: Mr Li. Did you see Mr Li?

Beat.

DWAYNE: I spoke to him.

SHANELL: You spoke to him? I thought you were going to see him! [*His focus is on the front door.*] Okay, okay. You chatted to him on the phone. And then?

DWAYNE: Gotta call him again tonight.

SHANELL: Ja, nice. What did he say? Today?

DWAYNE: He's interested.

SHANELL: Just interested?

DWAYNE [*angrily*]. What do you want me to say here, Shanell?

SHANELL [*sniping back*]: I want you to tell me he's buying that horn! That he's paying us a big fat fortune for it!

DWAYNE: If he's interested, he's buying. End of story.

SHANELL: Ja, but how can you be so sure?

DWAYNE [*exploding*]: Because that's how these Orientals operate, OK! They are not like bladdy Europeans, jumping up and down like maniacs every time something tit-hot-lekker pops up on their radar. Cool, calm and collected. And that's how we gonna be.

SHANELL: Okay, fine. [*She's on her way out.*] Your supper's in the warmer drawer.

DWAYNE gawks as she heads off.

DWAYNE: Where you going now?

SHANELL: Candice is in a total state. Greg beat her up and buggered off again.

DWAYNE: Yassas, Shanell! [*He shakes his head in disbelief.*] How many times must I tell you? The woman is not worth it.

SHANELL: That's your problem, Dwayne. To you, no woman is worth it.

Beat.

DWAYNE [*softening*]: When you be back?

SHANELL: I might … I might have to stay over. [*Beat.*] I'm sorry about your … [*She indicates his hand.*]

DWAYNE: Ag, my own fault. I was sloppy. [*He checks the hand.*] Fuck knows when I'll get the chance to nail him again.

He reaches for his brandy, which is on the desk.

SHANELL: Mrs de Freitas called. Says she's happy with her gate.

DWAYNE: At least somebody's happy.

He knocks back the brandy. SHANELL turns again to leave, guiltily drifting out. His voice stops her.

DWAYNE: Was she woes?

SHANELL [*turning back*]: Who? You mean, Mrs …

DWAYNE: When she rocked up and I wasn't here?

SHANELL: She was orraight. They got money, hey. She told me. Her husband's this Head kind of like Honcho. He's in with the Comrades.

DWAYNE: Comrades?

SHANELL: Something about politics … likes hearing skinner stories. She was one of those … what-do-they-call-them? When they stay overseas for a long time?

DWAYNE: She was in exile?

SHANELL: Ja. And you can mos hear she's not stupid, hey.

DWAYNE appears deeply preoccupied … during the above exchange he has moved slowly to Jonas's locker. He holds onto it and finally rests his head against it.

SHANELL [*baffled by this odd behaviour*]: Are you orraight?

DWAYNE: Huh?

SHANELL: We'll be able to get that headstone. When we

get the money for the ... we'll be able to get that
headstone for Jonas. Could get a whole pile of
headstones and still have enough.

DWAYNE: Ja.

SHANELL: You not to blame, you know.

DWAYNE: For what?

SHANELL: That night before he died.

DWAYNE: What about it?

SHANELL: You told him to stay. He wanted to go home.

DWAYNE: He didn't have to go home.

SHANELL: But he did. And the next day he was dead. But
he could have died anywhere, anytime ... crossing the
road ... accident with that blimmen angle-grinder ...
the welding torch. [*She snorts.*] Coulda' choked on a
chicken bone!

DWAYNE [*furious*]: Tell me something, are you pissed?

SHANELL: What?

DWAYNE [*indicating the wine bottle on the table*]: You klap
that bottle all on your own?

SHANELL: Don't be stupid now, man! She helped me! [*Beat.
He turns away.*] What is it with you all of a sudden?
It's kak! We both know it's kak! But ever since Jonas
died you've been, like ... I dunno. I want to say 'short
fuse', but there's no fuse at all, it's just – Boem! All the
time ... Boem! Boem! Boem!

DWAYNE: Go visit your sad little chommie, Shanell.

*She heads off and then turns at the door to give him
some parting advice.*

SHANELL: Life goes on, Dwayne. And we still gotta live it.

55

She leaves. DWAYNE *moves to the window, watching, then slowly moves to a shelf, pushes various bits of bric-a-brac aside and locates an old cigar box. Music folds in – Lelilungelo Ngelakho (In the Valley, We Sleep in the Valley) by the Soweto Gospel Choir. He opens the box and carefully removes an animal skin bracelet, trying it on his wrist before removing it again. He gazes at it, then stares out front, weeping, as the lights fade to scene-change mode.*

Scene 4

It is late on the following night.

Lights fade up and the office is empty, gloomy but for the moonlight that streams in through the Venetian blinds at the window. The music holds, full volume.

SHANELL enters via the alcove in the half-light. She is barefoot and dressed in revealing summer sleeping gear. She looks vulnerable. She taps away on her smart phone, sending WhatsApps and moving across to the car seat. Some reply she has received to her WhatsApp angers her and she slams her phone down on the makeshift coffee table. Looking at the locker, she moves towards it and then collects the key, which is stuck under her husband's desk, and unlocks the padlock. Quietly opening the locker, she removes the rhino horn as the music fades.

SHANELL carries the rhino horn to the car seat and puts it down, kneeling beside it. She appears mesmerised, transfixed. So focused is she on the horn that it is a good few moments before she becomes aware of the presence of her husband, also barefoot, who has appeared in the alcove, wearing an old T-shirt and tracksuit bottoms.

DWAYNE [*still half asleep*]: What the hell are you doing?
SHANELL [*startled, covering the horn*]: How can they …?
> They come with their rifles, their chainsaws, and …
> [*She is devastated.*] … what happens to the babies?
> [*She is mystified.*] What was Jonas doing with this?

Beat.

DWAYNE [*quietly*]: Maybe he was keeping it for someone.

SHANELL: Or he could have been waiting to take it to the sangoma to have it, sort of … whatever it is they do. You know what these people are like.

DWAYNE: These people? [*He snaps on the light, dead calm.*] I want you to put that thing back where you found it.

In the brief pause that follows, SHANELL's phone bleeps, a message has come in. She snatches up the phone and glances hurriedly at the screen.

SHANELL [*chuckling nervously*]: Like me, Candice can't sleep.

DWAYNE moves menacingly towards her. As she hides the phone beside her, he leans across her and picks up the rhino horn, carrying it back to the locker and securing the padlock, returning the key to its spot beneath the desk.

SHANELL [*staring at him, eyes blazing*]: How long have you hated me? [*No response.*] So long you can't even remember! [*DWAYNE is unmoved.*] It's like you look right through me … don't see me! Your eyes … even when we did it, they were searching for someone else!

DWAYNE: What kak you talking now?

SHANELL: That first time … my flat tyre. Benoni. You rescued me … took me to Vivien's 'cos I was late. All the women there said, 'you mad, Shanell, he's too old for you'. Even then … you did all the right things, made all the right moves. [*Bitterly.*] It was like … you just going through the motions.

DWAYNE [*bristling*]: Alcohol's hi-jacked your fucken brain, you know that?

SHANELL: You think a woman doesn't know it when a man doesn't love her?

DWAYNE: You saying I was having women on the side?

SHANELL [*gesturing towards the locker*]: Maybe it wasn't a woman!

DWAYNE: What?

SHANELL [*throwing a curveball*]: Do you love me?

DWAYNE: Hey?

SHANELL: Is it such a hard question? Yes or no?

DWAYNE: Of course I love you.

SHANELL: Jeez, say it like you mean it!

DWAYNE: What is this, Shanell?

SHANELL: You tell me. You call this a marriage? [*She gives him no time to respond.*] Our marriage is a bladdy joke, 'cept no one's laughing!

DWAYNE: Takes two to tango.

SHANELL: What? You blaming me now?

DWAYNE: We still together. We've stuck it out.

SHANELL [*eyes heavenward*]: Wow, I love that!

DWAYNE: What do you want from me, man?

SHANELL [*with feeling*]: You know what I want, Dwayne. I want some payback. I want what's coming to me.

DWAYNE: Ah, yassas!

SHANELL: This property's worth a fortune. It's zoned for – whats-it? – business! Light industry! [*She is in full flight.*] That, combined with all the money from the horn, we go down to Ballito and never look back!

DWAYNE: It's not as simple as us just selling the …

SHANELL [*exploding*]: Dwayne! That is the deal! Take it or leave it!
[*Beat.*] Now, if you'll excuse me, I'm going to bed with my fucking vibrator.

She sweeps out through the archway. DWAYNE moves to the car seat, slumps down and leans back, exhausted. SHANELL slowly returns, speaking as she enters …

SHANELL [*reconciliatory*]: Forgive me, my baby. [*Beat.*] I'm sorry … about what I said before I went out.

DWAYNE stares out front … the thousand-mile stare.

She moves across to him and furtively picks up her phone from the car seat.

SHANELL [*placing a hand on his thigh*]: It's gonna be good, Dwayne. I promise you. We leave this place behind … Jonas … Harry Serfontein … all the memories, good and bad … we start all over again. New beginning.

During the above speech she rises, removes Jonas's blanket from the back of the car seat and takes it to the locker, placing it on top of it.

SHANELL: Don't fall asleep here, you get a stiff neck.

She bends down to kiss him gently on the cheek. As she moves away to return to bed he reaches out and takes her hand, pulling her back and holding her fiercely to him. She does not resist but then breaks away and heads for the alcove .

DWAYNE: Shanell … [*She turns to look at him.*] I'm sorry.
SHANELL [*smiling softly*]: Apology accepted.

DWAYNE rises from the car seat and takes a step forward.

DWAYNE: No. You don't understand … there's no Vietnamese. No Mr Li. [*Beat.*] No chats on the phone … or plans to get things moving.

SHANELL [*in growing horror*]: But you said that …

DWAYNE: I lied. I lied to keep you sweet.

SHANELL [*eyes like daggers*]: You telling me that all of this time …

DWAYNE [*emphatic*]: I'm not selling that horn. Not now! Not ever!

There is a moment when anything might happen but instead of the cataclysmic explosion that DWAYNE fully expects, SHANELL, pale with white-hot fury, spins away and tears off through the alcove. DWAYNE, rudderless, swings around and strides to the locker. Taking down the blanket his wife had placed there only a few moments before he carefully places it over the back of the car seat again.

SHANELL reappears, bearing a hastily-packed kitbag. She has pulled on an old windcheater and slip-slops and brandishes her car keys … letting him have it with both barrels.

SHANELL: I dunno what it is with you and Jonas, or you and that fucking horn … [*Before he can speak …*] But, you don't sell it, you don't phone to tell me you got that money in your hand …

DWAYNE: Shanell …

SHANELL: Then this is the last time you'll ever see me, as God is my witness!

DWAYNE: Where you going now?

SHANELL: I'm going to Candice!

DWAYNE: At two o' clock in the morning!?

SHANELL: We finish! It's over!

DWAYNE: You can't go out dressed like that!

SHANELL, ice-cool, approaches him, smiling a chilling, deadly smile that cuts him to the core.

SHANELL: You dead to me. You pathetic piece a' shit, you dead to me. As much use to the human race as … how was my head to even waste my time?

She turns and heads off.

DWAYNE [*calling after her*]: Shanell …! Shanell …!

DWAYNE remains rooted to the spot, helpless to stop her leaving. Noticing his baseball bat in a drum near the vestibule he whips it up and lurches about the office, looking for something to smash. He finally lays into a tall filing cabinet that is partially visible beside the workbench in his workshop.

As he swings and hammers away, unleashing his pent-up fury, the haunting strains of Vusi Mahlasela's 'Mayibuye' folds in over the speakers.

With the music soaring higher, DWAYNE, off, continues trashing his workshop until he finally runs out of steam. The music holds, still rising.

The lights fade to scene-change mode.

Scene 5

Several days later. Early evening.

As the lights fade up the office looks much as it always has apart from several empty McDonald's and KFC boxes lying around. Jonas's blanket lies crumpled on the car seat, suggesting that DWAYNE *has been sleeping as well as eating here.*

The music continues as DWAYNE *appears in the alcove, freshly showered and groomed. He wears his 'special occasion smart shirt' and clean trousers. He adjusts the animal skin bracelet on his wrist and then spots his gun on his desk. Checking that the firearm is on safety he opens a top drawer and places it carefully inside and the music fades out. Noticing the takeaway boxes, he scoops them up, tossing them into the workshop before crossing to the mirror above the basin to check his appearance.*

The sound of a car we have heard before sends DWAYNE *into a mini panic. He grabs his brandy bottle and glass from the coffee table and places them beside the fridge. Moving swiftly to his desk, he removes a can of antiperspirant from a drawer, blasting under each arm before putting it back. He whips up a remote device and activates the lock to the outside security gate.* NAMHLA *soon appears in the doorway, stylishly dressed.*

DWAYNE: Come in, come in. Welcome. Make yourself at home.

Spotting a single forgotten takeaway box, he kicks it swiftly beneath his desk. His current 'bachelor-like' existence does not go unnoticed.

NAMHLA [*ultra-cool*]: How's your wife? I trust she's well?

DWAYNE [*flustered*]: Ja, no … she's … she's lekker, she's …

NAMHLA: Not in tonight?

DWAYNE: Gone to a movie with her friend in town. [*A trifle too smarmy.*] Smart move, don't you think?

NAMHLA: Depends.

DWAYNE [*momentarily thrown*]: Sorry?

NAMHLA: I said it depends.

DWAYNE: On what?

NAMHLA: On what you have in mind.

Beat.

DWAYNE [*warily*]: We discussing the debt you want me to collect.

NAMHLA: You're sure about that?

DWAYNE: Of course. Unless …

NAMHLA: Unless?

Beat.

DWAYNE [*sly smile*]: You're a cagey one, you know that?

NAMHLA: Interesting. 'Cagey' would be my assessment of you.

DWAYNE: How so?

NAMHLA: The way you look at me. [*She pauses for effect.*] The way you've looked at me from the very first moment you saw me.

DWAYNE [*laughing a little too forcefully*]: No, no, no …
listen … me, I'm bok for anything, hey. But you
reading this all wrong.

NAMHLA [*totally unfazed*]: You're going to tell me you're
not like that?

DWAYNE: No Ways. At the same time, I'm not gonna lie to
you and say my marriage is one made in heaven. But I
know where's that line in the sand.

NAMHLA [*chuckling mirthlessly*]: Hah!

DWAYNE: What?

NAMHLA: The idea that a man, any man … particularly a
man as painfully obvious as you, can talk of lines in
the sand.

DWAYNE: I have my principles.

NAMHLA: I'd argue that point. [*She moves to his desk
and sits down in his chair.*] This debt collecting, for
example. You never stop to ask yourself whether it
might be a tad unethical?

*She brandishes the baseball bat, which is lying on his
desk.*

DWAYNE: People owe, they must pay.

NAMHLA: And you're the self-appointed judge and jury. No
questions asked.

DWAYNE: There's questions, of course. Like with you. I'd
have to know Who, Why, What and Where.

NAMHLA: Tick all the boxes.

DWAYNE: A lot of people they come to me, a lot of people I
turn them away. You might be one of them.

NAMHLA: I'll walk out of here disappointed?

DWAYNE: There's that possibility, ja … but I reckon things are gonna click into gear just fine. [*Quick change, a huge need to lighten things up.*] Listen, can I offer you something to drink?

NAMHLA: Water would be nice. Thank you.

DWAYNE: Water? [*He's thrown.*] Fixed up. [*He heads for the fridge.*] You mind tap? It's on tap, but it's chilled.

Chuckling at his own joke DWAYNE *sets about removing a grubby plastic bottle of tap water from the fridge and pouring a glass for his guest, all the while crooning for her benefit.*

DWAYNE [*sings*]: 'I found my thrill … on Blueberry Hill … on Blueberry Hill …'

Beat.

NAMHLA: Is that your happy song?

DWAYNE: Sorry?

He crosses to her.

NAMHLA: Your wife told me that you and your assistant sang little else.

DWAYNE: Ja … [*He chuckles.*] Blueberry Hill.

He hands her the glass of water.

NAMHLA [*taking the glass*]: Thank you. Any particular reason? That song, I mean.

DWAYNE: It was our place.

NAMHLA [*nodding, getting it*]: A time and a place.

DWAYNE: No, no … this was a real place … the place I first met ol' Jonas. [*Beat.*] I had this mad Scottish uncle down in the Lowveld … my mother's brother. He was a farmer. [*He snorts.*] Well, fancied himself as a farmer. For years he'd been searching for that perfect pozzie. Became something of a family joke, Uncle Roydon looking for his little piece of Africa. [*He chuckles.*] Anyway, so one day he sees this ad in the paper for this small farm somewhere near Nelspruit. It's called Blueberry Hill. Wham-Bam – sight unseen he puts in this offer.

NAMHLA: Hasn't seen it?

DWAYNE: Hey, it's gotta be tit-hot-lekker, right? He's getting these pictures in his brain of like heaven-on-earth, all-things-bright-and-beautiful.

NAMHLA: Lovely.

DWAYNE: Lovely, ja … until he finally gets down there. [*He's amused.*] Surprise, surprise! No hill … no blueberries … no boggerol. Just thorn trees, those vicious bastards. Wag-a-bietjie bome on steroids. [*He gurgles.*] Turns out the bloke who had the place before him just happened to like the bladdy song.

NAMHLA [*smiling*]: Wicked.

DWAYNE: Listen, I'm just going to sort myself out here. Osso need a … [*He heads across to the fridge again, fixing himself a double brandy and still chuckling away.*]
Gotta hand it to him, hey, my uncle. Finally tamed that piece a' land and made a go of it.

NAMHLA [*probing*]: So, this … Jonas. You were teenagers when you first met?

DWAYNE: One school holiday, ja. [*He returns with his drink.*] He was down at the river making kleilatte.

You know, those lumps of clay? [*He demonstrates.*]
Whipping them across the water … Shhoeff! [*He
speaks as though it was yesterday.*] Black oukie …
coupla' years older than me in this white shirt. [*He
mimes whipping the clay ball across the river.*] Shhoeff!
Pow-pow-pow-powww!

NAMHLA [*half to herself*]: Had to be a white shirt.

DWAYNE [*distracted*]: Sorry?

NAMHLA: No, I was … the white shirt …

DWAYNE: What about it?

NAMHLA: I'm fascinated it was his white shirt that caught
your attention.

He waits for her to continue, eyes boring into her.

DWAYNE: She told you, didn't she? [*Her look confirms it.*]
[*Beat.*] My bladdy wife talks too much.

NAMHLA: It just came out. It wasn't planned.

DWAYNE: What else she tell you?

NAMHLA: Not much.

DWAYNE: Not much?

NAMHLA: She told me … she told me the story about your
father … when you were a small boy, driving in that
car and shooting at those … [*She gets to the point.*]
She told me that you thought you'd …

DWAYNE: That I'd killed somebody.

NAMHLA: Yes, and then you … searched for the … You went
to the hospital and the township, and … all the rest of it.

Beat.

DWAYNE [*muttering*]: Nothing sacred anymore. [*He puts
down his brandy and moves behind the car seat, gazing*

out of the window, haunted.] Never goes away … the hope that maybe one day … [*Beat.*] I see a black man in a white shirt and there's that … moment. [*He moves towards her, unguished.*] And then there's times I find him, you know, at night in my dreams. Sometimes he's dead and I bury him. Sometimes he's wounded and I fix him up, take him home to his wife and kids, who still waiting for him. Sometimes … sometimes I find his mother and she's putting flowers on his grave. I tell her what happened … that it was me who did this … it was me that killed her son.

NAMHLA: And she forgives you?

DWAYNE [*achingly desperate*]: I never know. Because it's in the moment her eyes look into mine I always wake up.

There is a brief pause … a deep, distant, faraway roll of thunder, a Highveld storm in the offing. It fades away.

NAMHLA: There is a chance he survived. The possibility that …

DWAYNE [*snorts*]: Possibility! Chance! Just now you gonna tell me what's done is done. [*A wild anger.*] The past is never past … it chases after you like a starving beast … stop, you get torn to pieces!

There is another roll of thunder, a little more ominous than the first.

DWAYNE *switches on the lights near the vestibule as darkness closes in.*

DWAYNE [*pulling himself together*]: OK. Come on. We gonna sort you out, better get this show on the road.

He crosses to his desk for a pen and a notebook.
NAMHLA *studies him carefully. The probing continues.*

NAMHLA: Are you quite sure you're up for this?

DWAYNE [*thrown*]: Up for what?

NAMHLA: Hunting down the man that owes me so much.

Beat.

DWAYNE [*sheepish chuckle*]: OK. Orraight. Kick a oke when he's down. But that little hiccup you witnessed last time you were here … [*he raises the baseball bat*] … done and dusted.

NAMHLA: You smash his head in?

DWAYNE: Sadly, not. But the debt's been paid in full.

NAMHLA: Wouldn't it be marvellous if all debts could end up fully settled.

DWAYNE [*smiling as though he's experienced this*]: Oh, they always are … one way or another. The Indians call it karma.

NAMHLA: Karma?

DWAYNE: You get what's coming to you, no matter how much you duck and dive.

A beat. The telephone on the desk rings. DWAYNE *gives his guest a resigned look and picks up the receiver.*

DWAYNE: Ja …? [*He rolls his eyes.*] Oh, ja, howzit? [*He ducks into the alcove.*] No, I'm lekker … I thought you-me we s'posed to be history. [*He is flustered.*] What? No, I am not thinking again of tryna' sell the …! Ridgely? Who the fuck is Ridgely? [*He emerges from the alcove.*] No, no, no, no, no! I've told you,

Shanell, there is nothing to discuss! [*His anger builds.*] Stop shouting! Ja, ja … stop shouting, man, for fucksake! [*He grimaces.*] Yassas, Shanell, if you don't …! [*He yanks the phone away from his ear and stabs away at it until he hits the 'end call' button.*] Fuckit! [*Throwing the phone onto the desk he yells at it. He is apoplectic.*]

Ridgely! What kind of a doosagtige name is that?

NAMHLA is staring at him and DWAYNE suddenly becomes aware of his crazy behaviour.

DWAYNE: I'm sorry about, er … [*He indicates the phone.*] That was …

NAMHLA: I heard.

A pause. DWAYNE knows the cat is out of the bag with respect to his wife.

DWAYNE: Look, I … er … I spun you a little bit of a white lie tonight. [*Beat.*] I told you my wife had gone to a movie. Truth is …

NAMHLA [*matter of factly*]: She's left you.

DWAYNE: She's grabbed her stuff, she's out the house.

Beat.

NAMHLA: When did this happen?

DWAYNE: Ag, four-five days orreadly.

NAMHLA: I'm sorry.

DWAYNE: I'm not. I'm just surprised it's taken so long. [*Beat.*] S'pose it's a bit of a miracle, considering …

NAMHLA: Considering?

DWAYNE: The rocky ride. [*His tone is bitter.*] The so-called …
indiscretions. Our marriage made a tsunami look like a
ripple in a bird bath.

*He bursts out laughing, finding something very funny
indeed.*

NAMHLA: Are you all right?

DWAYNE: Candice Wolmerans! [*He heads across to the
front door.*] Every time she's out the house to go meet
Candice Wolmerans, I'm going … 'ja, pull the other
one'. [*He is seething.*] Ridgely! Tit-hot name for a
toyboy, hey. A name like that, she's welcome to him.
[*He yells out of the window and swoops on his brandy
bottle.*] Probably some tattooed little windgat from
Springs or Nigel … drives around in a Golf GTi with
a piss-will spoiler and mag wheels. [*He gulps straight
from the bottle and then realises what this must
look like and apologises.*] Oh, hell … sorry! Sorry!
Dammit! [*He swiftly puts the bottle back and picks up
the pen and notebook from the desk.*] Right. C'mon.
Who's now this snake in the grass we looking for?

*The approaching storm grows louder as another roll of
thunder is heard. The sound is closer, angrier … a clap
of thunder and the lights flicker.*

DWAYNE [*reacting to the storm*]: Whooah! Fire and Ice.
Good thing you got your wheels under the afdak
outside there.

Another deep, angry roar. It fades away.

NAMHLA: I still can't get used to that. [*She moves to the window.*] You spend all those years in England, it's easy to forget. Tied to my mother's back in a blanket … thunder and lightning all around. Her, running like mad for the nearest shelter and those raindrops like angry pebbles on top of my head.

Beat. DWAYNE *places the pen and notebook back on the desk.*

DWAYNE: When did you leave?
NAMHLA: This country? [*She still clearly feels the pain.*] A long time ago.

He crosses to her and sits on the car seat while she remains standing behind it.

DWAYNE: I'd count my blessings. This place was no picnic.
NAMHLA: Picnic or not, there's still a part of me that feels cheated.
DWAYNE: Wouldn't say that if you spent half your life in Ogies.
NAMHLA: The town where you grew up?
DWAYNE: Means 'eyes' in Afrikaans. They say a man born in Ogies sees everything. [*He chuckles hollowly.*] Pity I didn't see the trap lying in wait for me.
NAMHLA: Trap?
DWAYNE: Leaving school. Clever me, I joined the police force to avoid going to the Border. [*He snorts.*] So much for circumnavigating the kak.

She stares at him with a mixture of fascination and incredulity.

73

NAMHLA: This is bizarre! [*Beat.*] I'm having a drink and chat with a man who …

DWAYNE: With a man who was once an apartheid policeman. [*Beat.*] What is it you wanna know? [*His tone is quietly menacing.*] That we went out in the dead a' night? Kicked down doors in the townships at four in the morning?

Beat.

NAMHLA: You actually did that?

DWAYNE: What do you think?

NAMHLA: I'm asking you.

DWAYNE: Ja, well, I got a question for you. [*He gets to his feet.*] Why does a woman with connections come all away to the Far East Rand to hunt for something she could get in her own back yard? If it's true your husband is in with the Comrades, you sure as hell don't need Dwayne Arthur Combrink.

NAMHLA [*drippingly sarcastic*]: No? I heard his reputation was second to none.

Beat.

DWAYNE [*his brain going every which way*]: Are you taking the piss?

NAMHLA: Is that what you think?

DWAYNE: I dunno what to think. All I know is, I look at this person …

NAMHLA: This person …

DWAYNE: This person, ja. I'm thinking there's something about her …

NAMHLA: Who is she?

DWAYNE: Who is she? Exactly.

NAMHLA: That's a question she keeps asking herself all the time. Head in England, heart over here. Who she is, is lost in the gap in between!

DWAYNE is taken aback by her reaction. There is another distant rumble of thunder. He moves to the coffee-table crate and sits down on it. NAMHLA watches him.

NAMHLA: Nineteen-eighty. The year we left. I was four years old. [*Beat.*] You tell people in England you were born on the 16th of June, 1976 … it means nothing at all to them.

DWAYNE [*snorts, quietly*]: Not to those who were there.

NAMHLA: Auspicious, my father called it. I was his Child of the Revolution.

Beat.

DWAYNE [*grunting wryly*]: On the day you were born I was rumbling into Soweto in the belly of a Hippo … twenty-two years old … rifle in hand … heart in my mouth. [*He paces about.*] All I could think of was why don't these kids just sommer go back in their houses? Drop their sticks, their stones, stop their chanting, and … [*He is clearly back there again.*] Anger has a smell … burning tyres, black smoke. Sits in the back a' your throat like it's never going away. [*A beat and he snaps out of it.*] Sorry, you were saying?

NAMHLA [*momentarily thrown*]: I was saying?

DWAYNE: Your father?

NAMHLA: My father, yes. He was a teacher … an activist.

DWAYNE: A so-called 'troublemaker'?

NAMHLA: When he slipped out of the country nearly two years later my mother thought we'd never see him again. [*Beat.*] I turned three, I turned four, and all I knew of this man was that he was fighting for our Freedom. What Freedom meant to a child my age heaven alone knows. My aunt said, 'you watch … he'll come home one day, carried high on the shoulders of his Comrades … singing songs and waving flags'.

DWAYNE: And your mother … she never believed that?

NAMHLA: She believed that Freedom was coming, absolutely … but seeing my father again …? [*Bitter-sweet, it still gets her.*] She always loved the fact it was Wally Serote paved the way.

DWAYNE: Wally Serote?

NAMHLA: The poet. Who, in turn, led her to Max Weinstein. [*Beat.*] They met at a poetry evening. He and his family lived in Oaklands somewhere … Orchards. Max hated the apartheid regime almost as much as my mother did. He'd tell her stories of Berlin … how his parents had been killed by Hitler in the Holocaust … said he'd never let that happen to us … said a family needed to stay together because you never know when that axe might fall. [*Beat.*]
  And then one day he just came out with it … the plan to get us to England.

DWAYNE: You mean he, like …?

NAMHLA: Collected money … organised false passports … sent messages across to my father, and him all the time saying it was far too dangerous. [*Wry chuckle.*]

What was so dangerous about going on a little holiday?

DWAYNE: Swaziland?

NAMHLA: Lesotho. Me, my mother, the Weinsteins and their son, a couple of years older than me. [*She chortles.*] We kids were completely unaware of all the behind-the-scenes stuff. We were off to the mountains to splash about in the waterfalls, ride ponies. [*Beat.*] When the day arrived everything changed. [*She recalls it all too well.*] That journey in the car, so long and hot … the fear … the trepidation. My mother humming lullabies to calm her nerves. Max and his wife growing ever more silent. And then there we were … pulling up at that border post … four ordinary people playing Happy Families.

DWAYNE [*confused … there were five of them*]: Four?

NAMHLA: I was out of sight, hiding under my mother's long dress on the floor, trying not to breathe. This customs official was staring at her … she thought the game was up. And then he gave Max this knowing smile. What a smart thing to do, he said, going on holiday and taking the kaffir-maid along. [*Beat.*] And that was that. [*She chuckles ironically.*] Looking back, it just had to be normal – kosher, as Max's wife would say. Mum and dad, obedient black nursemaid, taking care of their precious little 'boychik'. All very … South African.

DWAYNE [*simultaneously*]: South African.

Beat.

NAMHLA: Young as I was, the picture's still crystal clear. Mr Weinstein at that airport as they waved us goodbye … weeping … sobbing … like the dam had finally burst. He couldn't save his parents from the Nazis, but this he could do. A mother, a daughter … not even his own.

DWAYNE [*deeply moved*]: And your father in England? He was waiting?

NAMHLA: When we landed at Heathrow it was the happiest day of my life. We hadn't seen him in two years and he'd grown older and thinner, his lungs giving in. Not that we knew this. He was my dad. We were together again … and that was all that mattered.

Thunder rolls closer … deep, ominous … DWAYNE looks heavenward.

DWAYNE [*trying to break sombre mood*]: Mother Nature, clearing her throat. [*Beat.*] Old Jonas … he always said that … storm coming.

NAMHLA [*looking at him grimly*]: Max Weinstein's good deed didn't go unpunished. The Security Branch raided his house … ninety days behind bars … interrogated … tortured. [*The debt lies heavy.*] They say when he came out he was never the same.

DWAYNE [*quietly, with more than a twinge of guilt*]: There were white people, ja … stuck their necks out … paid the price. Shame on those of us who stood back.

NAMHLA studies this man who appears to hide behind his mask so cunningly.

NAMHLA: It must've been quite an adjustment for you … the whole … transition.

DWAYNE: Transition?

NAMHLA: Your way of life … when it all … nineteen-ninety-four, I mean.

DWAYNE: It was a change, ja.

NAMHLA: You weren't affected? No sense of … loss, regret?

DWAYNE: Ag, you roll with the punches. I do. Always have. Anyway, I'm too old now to worry about what was. Madiba's come and gone, and … hey, what do you know? I'm still here.

NAMHLA: So you're fine the way things are?

DWAYNE [*stung*]: What kinda' question's that?

NAMHLA: Is it corruption? Affirmative action? The fact that for a white male who once had everything on a plate …

DWAYNE: Lady, please. I don't want to get into all of this, OK?

NAMHLA: Of course you don't. You've had it good. You want it to stay that way. You're not still waiting for that one moment deep in your heart when at last … please, God! … longing gives way to be-longing.

DWAYNE *cannot help but notice her sudden mood swing. Her deep pain and anger over aspirations not realised.*

NAMHLA: Twenty years. [*She still can't believe it.*] Half a lifetime on that side, the other half … where? In limbo! Because that's what it feels like. [*Beat.*] You have these images in your head of what it might be like coming home, but you really have no clue. It's all fantasy. Nostalgia doesn't come into it because you were far too young to remember … and slowly you begin to realise that the dreams you believed were your dreams, are actually second-hand … passed down by your parents, their Comrades. But now you're eighteen years old and here you are. You feel duty bound to embrace your culture, your homeland … after all, it's what's expected of you. But nothing's familiar, nothing … connects. And so you do your best to join in. You pretend. And the more you pretend the more disengaged you feel. Alienated. You're an alien.

DWAYNE: So what you saying is … your real home's in England?

NAMHLA: Yes. No! I don't know. Age four to eighteen is a lifetime! [*It's as though she's accusing him.*] When your childhood is stolen, you can never get it back!

DWAYNE [*bitterly*]: Tell me about it! Except in my case it was my old man stole mine. You were an alien, I was a zombie. We all got our stuff.

NAMHLA [*wondering where this is coming from*]: Our stuff?

DWAYNE [*becoming quite animated*]: Our stuff, ja. The stuff that comes along when you living in this world.

NAMHLA: Good God! [*Bitterly.*] You're not equating your life with mine?

DWAYNE: Get one thing straight. I didn't steal nothing from you.

NAMHLA: No? Mr Ex-policeman!

DWAYNE [*finally cracking*]: Yes! Orraight! Enough! Guilty as Charged! I didn't have the guts to take a stand against injustice! All I can do now is damn well live with it!

NAMHLA [*a grenade*]: And can you live with what you did to Rebecca Sangweni?

The mention of this name stops DWAYNE *in his tracks. Everything has changed.*

NAMHLA [*unrelenting*]: Was it common practice in those days to treat domestic workers as concubines? [*Responding to his shattered look.*] To use them and abuse them and then toss them out like soiled goods?

Beat.

DWAYNE [*shocked, bewildered*]: Who the hell are you?

NAMHLA: Apartheid had other perks and they weren't just the obvious ones.

DWAYNE: How dare you!

NAMHLA: Oh, I dare all right.

DWAYNE: Where you come with this?

NAMHLA: Butter wouldn't melt.

DWAYNE: You a journalist? You a reporter? [*He is distraught, his anger rising.*] You pick up some stompie of a story somewhere, and …

NAMHLA: Do you deny that you had a black domestic worker living on your …

DWAYNE: Jonas! Did Jonas tell you this?

NAMHLA: I don't know Jonas. I've never known a Jonas.

DWAYNE [*with a mixture of hope and desperation*]: Where is she?

NAMHLA: Where is she?

DWAYNE: Is she …? Is she still …?

NAMHLA: Don't you think it's a bit late for that? [*He is hurt.*] The woman is dead!

The impertinence … the insensitivity … it is all too much for DWAYNE.

DWAYNE: Get outa' my house! Get the fuck outa' my house!

NAMHLA: Still can't admit to it.

DWAYNE: Parasites …!

NAMHLA: Oppressor turned victim.

DWAYNE [*spitting it out*]: You people who feed on the misery of others … dig up dirt, make up stories, fill your vile books with vomit and then sit back and …

NAMHLA: You think that's what this is all about?

DWAYNE [*exploding*]: Rebecca Sangweni was the love of my life! Thabisa was everything to me! The sun, the moon, the stars …! [*His tirade is interrupted by a crash of thunder and bright flashes of lightning.*] Jonas Nhlapo was not the only person I met on Blueberry Hill. [*Anguished.*] Would that he was.

DWAYNE spins away and paces about, ending up at the locker in the mouth of the workshop, his back to her, staring into the gloomy interior. There is another deep rumble of thunder … a strobe-flicker of lightning.

NAMHLA is silent now as she watches him. After a long pause DWAYNE breaks away from the workshop, studies her briefly and then, slowly, quietly, opens up. It is a bitter-sweet release for him as he shares his tale for the first time.

DWAYNE [*for him it still seems like yesterday*]: She was a student at university … Turfloop … on one of those

… middla' the year vacations. [*He snorts.*] Way out
of my league. All I knew is that there she was in this
sad excuse for a school classroom – broken windows,
no desks … reading out loud to these barefoot kids
as wide-eyed and breathless as I was. [*He recalls the
scene fondly.*] What a piece of work is man … how
noble in reason, how … all that stuff about angels and
gods and beauty and when she looked up … [*He darts
around his desk.*] I was outa' there so quick. Jonas saw
the whole thing and he oready knew. Her eyes, he
said … with her eyes Thabisa Sangweni has captured
your heart. [*Beat. He slams his fist on the desk.*] It was
wrong. It was right, but it was osso wrong. All the
time my brain was saying 'no', but in my heart … I
knew. And so did she. [*Beat. He indicates the locker.*]
He set up that first meeting. We could never have
done it ourselves, we were far too shy, both of us.
There in the boma, in the firelight, he left us alone.
[*He smiles.*] What to talk about? Each time one of us
tried to say something, the other would speak.

NAMHLA [*simultaneously*]: The other would speak.

*He looks at her, then drifts across to the window and
gazes out through the blinds.*

DWAYNE: And then those long months in between …
meeting up again on that farm … not a hope in hell
… our families, this country! [*Bitter-sweet laugh.*]
But nothing's impossible when two hearts are like
this! [*He brings both hands together. A beat.*] It wasn't
easy. The life we lived and the life we showed to the
world. When we came up here from the Lowveld we

had to find a place that was out of the way. Where things could appear … [*rueful snort*] … huh … 'normal'. The master, his right-hand man and the professor-to-be, posing as a house maid. [*He shakes his head.*] It was madness! Under the radar … smoke and mirrors … [*bitterly*] … Love like an assegai, the one side smooth, shiny, reassuring … and then the blade, cutting deep.

NAMHLA: Did anyone … ever …?

DWAYNE: Oh, there were rumours … suspicions … people on the plots giving you those looks. Thabisa was convinced that any night our front door was gonna burst from its hinges and in they'd come … the dogs, the torches, the guns … [*He snarls at the bitter irony.*] My comrades-in-arms. [*Beat. He is heartbroken.*] I shoulda' known it couldn't last. The morning I woke up and found her gone was the worst day of my life. No letter … no note. All I could do was go out and look … keep looking … until it finally came to me she was never coming back. [*He is weeping now.*] And Jonas? [*He snorts wryly.*] I think he was relieved. He always swore that it was going to end bad, that someone was going to get hurt. Hurt! As if anything could hurt more than her leaving!

A pause as NAMHLA *tries to process story.* DWAYNE'S *tone is measured.*

DWAYNE: So please tell me now … what became of your mother?

Beat.

84

NAMHLA: Nothing would make me happier than to tell you that she was still alive and thriving. [*She cuts to the chase.*] She died eight years ago. [*Beat.*] When did it dawn on you that I was her daughter?

DWAYNE: I should of realised the moment I first saw you, the day I came in from the workshop … you standing there. Your eyes, the tilt of your head. Every moment you've been here, it's like … that time coming back. [*He stares at her.*] Tonight, when you spoke her name … [*Words fail him.*]

Beat.

NAMHLA: The number of times I drove past here … slowing down … waiting to see what he looked like … this white man.

DWAYNE: She told you about me?

NAMHLA: Not a word. I'd never have known of your existence if it hadn't been for … [*She stops, suddenly feeling the urge to flee.*] This is all too confusing, it's … [*She turns on him.*] What proof do I have you're not lying? Not whitewashing the past! All that you've told me is nothing like what her sister described to me.

DWAYNE: Her sister?

NAMHLA: It's why I'm here.

DWAYNE [*spitting out the name*]: Nomzamo!

NAMHLA: You knew her?

DWAYNE: And how! She could never stomach this umlungu!

NAMHLA: Three months ago my aunt was on her deathbed. She told me there were things about my mother's life that I needed to know … how she was raped and

85

molested by the white man who worked with iron and steel.

DWAYNE: 'Raped … molested …' [*He shakes his head grimly.*]

NAMHLA: She told me where you lived.

DWAYNE: So it's this woman's word against mine? [*He is angry and disillusioned.*] Lies upon lies, and yours included.

NAMHLA: What do you mean?

A sharp clap of thunder, a flash of lightning. The storm finally breaks and rain pounds on the corrugated iron roof, growing ever louder.

DWAYNE: A writer takes liberties for the sake of a good story … ja, fine! [*He drives it home.*] You osso have to do that when it comes to your own life?

NAMHLA: I don't know what you're talking about …

DWAYNE: And this father in exile, so proud of his daughter … his Child of the Revolution. [*She turns away.*] And then the biggest lie of all … that you were born on Youth Day, on June 16, 1976.

NAMHLA: It's the truth!

DWAYNE: If it's the truth, then please explain it to me! [*His grenade.*] Your mother walked out of my life in November of '75. How is it possible that …?

In a cataclysm of thunder and lightning the storm reaches its zenith, drowning out all other sound. DWAYNE backs away from the woman he now realises could well be his daughter. The storm rages on, subsiding eventually to the odd few drops of rain on the roof. Silence. A long pause.

DWAYNE [*not looking at her*]: Always so quiet after the rain.

She is watching him keenly as he focuses on the ceiling, on anything but her.

NAMHLA: That's all you can say? [*In the centre of the office, water drip-drips to the floor from a leak in the roof.* Is it so hard now to look at me? [*DWAYNE grabs the bucket from beneath the basin and places it in the centre of the room. The metronomic drips continue. NAMHLA ploughs on.*] There was something else my aunt told me before she died. That the wonderful, caring man I'd always believed to be my beloved father was, in fact, my stepfather. [*DWAYNE cannot look at her, his mind is in turmoil.*] I refused to accept it. Even all those months afterwards when I finally plucked up the courage to come here … look you straight in the eye … [*DWAYNE's eyes scour the ceiling as he desperately searches for another drip.*] That night when you came in here bleeding … your blood on my handkerchief … I couldn't believe I was actually doing it … getting home … looking up ways on the internet to … I called in a favour from one of Lanford's connections. [*She removes the written proof from her handbag.*] It took three days for the DNA results to come back. Conclusive. No shadow of a doubt. [*Beat.*] Will you look at me! [*She explodes.*] I said look at me! [*DWAYNE either cannot or will not do as she asks.*] I had a gun in my bag on our first meeting. [*He still will not look at her.*] If I had found you alone I was going to shoot you.

DWAYNE [*lashing out*]: Well, why didn't you?

NAMHLA [*heartfelt*]: Because it's not an easy thing to do, kill your own father.

The sound of the storm retreating. DWAYNE takes a step towards his daughter.

DWAYNE [*lost, bewildered*]: My child …

NAMHLA: You think it's like some bad spell's been broken? [*A deep, wild anger.*] That suddenly, miraculously, I'm your daughter?

DWAYNE [*mortified*]: I didn't know! Please forgive me! When I saw you, I saw my Thabisa … that's why I made advances.

NAMHLA [*again wanting to flee*]: I have to go.

She turns to leave.

DWAYNE: No! Please.

NAMHLA [*spinning round to face him*]: What? You want to … what? Sit around and talk about … what? My life? My mother's?

DWAYNE [*punch-drunk*]: I had nightmares all the time … her wandering the streets … lost, alone. [*He is awestruck.*] She only left me … to protect me!

NAMHLA [*desperate*]: You never hurt her?

DWAYNE: Sweet Jesus.

He swings away.

NAMHLA: You swear that all that you've told me is true.

DWAYNE: As God is my Witness!

A long pause. The drip-drip-drip from the leak in the roof into the bucket is like the ticking of a clock. They're together and a thousand miles apart.

NAMHLA [*gently*]: You really ought to do something about your roof.

She turns to leave. DWAYNE cannot bear to see her go.

DWAYNE [*desperate*]: Wait! Her bracelet! This is her bracelet. [*He raises his arm to show her.*] She gave it to me as a mark of our union!

NAMHLA [*with all the tenderness she can muster*]: Look after yourself.

Before she can turn again to leave, his voice stops her.

DWAYNE: Namhla … ! What was it like? What was she like …? Was she …?

She studies this sad, lost soul for a while … this man who loved and lost his woman.

NAMHLA: I have a photograph.

DWAYNE: A picture? You have a picture?

She opens her handbag and begins scratching around inside it.

NAMHLA: I keep a couple in my handbag.

DWAYNE: I had a picture of the two of us, taken by Jonas … kept it at his place … [*grimly*] … before they flattened it!

Over the next line comes the sound of a car approaching at speed.

NAMHLA [*searching fruitlessly*]: Urgh! Honestly! [*She is frustrated.*] This is …

DWAYNE [*pointing to the handbag*]: Look! Keep looking!

NAMHLA [*digging, muttering*]: Got so many bags, it's no wonder I can't …

*The vehicle grinds to a halt in a shower of stones
outside and the powerful headlights that spear in
through the blinds are snapped off … the engine is
killed.*

DWAYNE [*glancing briefly at the window*]: What the …?

NAMHLA [*Giving up, apologetic*]: I'm sorry. This is crazy.
I've got so many photographs of my mother at home
… shoe boxes … whole albums …

*In no time at all a hyped-up, hugely excited SHANELL
hurtles into the office. She wears a flashy leather
jacket and tight jeans – yet again, mutton-dressed-as
lamb, only more so. She ignores NAMHLA completely,
enthusiastically addressing the man she so recently
walked out on.*

SHANELL [*eyes blazing with wild intensity*]: It's fantastic! All
sorted! Ridgely's found someone who'll take it!

DWAYNE [*bursting with pride*]: Shanell, how's this? I have a
daughter!

SHANELL: The horn! We found a buyer!

DWAYNE: It's Namhla. Namhla's my daughter!

SHANELL: Bladdy hell, Dwayne, are you listening to me?
Ridgley's got hold of this Chinese. He's got the money.
He'll pay what we ask!

Beat.

DWAYNE [*glancing quickly at the window*]: Don't fucking
believe this.

*He strides purposefully for the baseball bat that still lies
on his desk.*

SHANELL: Believe it, Dwayne, it's true! We rich! We can make a plan …

DWAYNE [*grabbing the bat*]: A plan!

SHANELL: Yes! Do a deal. Ridgley's happy with only a small-tiny cut.

DWAYNE: This Ridgely … he's outside?

SHANELL: Yes. He's in the car. [*Hope springs eternal.*] You wanna meet him?

DWAYNE: Bladdy sure I wanna meet him!

He strides towards the front door, brandishing the bat.

SHANELL: Dwayne, listen …

DWAYNE [*turning back to her, over-excited*]: C'mon …! Let's go talk!

SHANELL is going nowhere … she rips open the top drawer of the desk and whips out DWAYNE's firearm. Clutching it with both hands she points it directly at him.

NAMHLA [*aghast*]: Oh, my oath!

SHANELL [*on the edge now, unravelling*]: I didn't want it to be like this! Ridgely says we here for that horn, we not leaving without it.

DWAYNE, amused at this turn of events, tosses his bat onto the car seat.

DWAYNE [*chuckling sardonically*]: You might want to check it's not on safety.

SHANELL: This is no time for jokes! Gimme the bladdy thing!

The safety catch is off.

DWAYNE [*slowly advancing on her, unfazed*]: I can't do that, Shanell.

SHANELL: You can and you will!

She retreats, still pointing the gun at him.

NAMHLA [*desperate*]: Shanell, please …

SHANELL: Shaddap! Who asked you?

DWAYNE: I told you before, my baby …

SHANELL: Ja, ja, ja … the fucking horn belongs to a dead man! You be dead if you don't give it to me right now!

DWAYNE: I don't have it.

SHANELL [*stunned, confused*]: What do you mean you don't have it?

DWAYNE: Last week orready … threw it in the middla' Boksburg Lake.

SHANELL: You lie …! [*She freaks out.*] Nobody would be so bladdy stupid!

He is already heading casually towards the locker, which now has no padlock.

DWAYNE [*swinging open the locker door*]: You wanna check … feel free.

He smiles as he walks away from the locker, his back to his wife. SHANELL moves across to the locker and sees that, indeed, there is no horn inside.

SHANELL screams, causing DWAYNE to swing around. She is already firing … three haphazard shots in his direction. NAMHLA ducks behind the car seat. SHANELL, still screaming, drops the gun on the desk and flees. There is the sound of a car door slamming, an engine bursting into life, headlights are switched on and a vehicle tears off into the night.

DWAYNE has not moved. NAMHLA, rising from behind the car seat, stares at him.

NAMHLA [*tremulous*]: Are you all right?

DWAYNE [*smiling, unfazed*]: She'd win boggerol prizes at a target shoot.

DWAYNE leans against his desk, clutching at his side with his bandaged hand.

NAMHLA [*dazed, confused*]: The horn ... that horn ... what was she talking about?

DWAYNE: Wanted something for mahala ... something that wasn't hers to have.

An anxious NAMHLA glances off. DWAYNE has other concerns.

DWAYNE: Listen ... you wanna check again? The pictures ...

NAMHLA: Pictures?

DWAYNE: In your... [*He indicates her handbag.*]

NAMHLA: I could've sworn I had them on me. [*She is mortified.*] I'm so sorry.

Beat.

DWAYNE [*wincing*]: I'd really like to see them.

NAMHLA: Yes, of course ... [*She notices his painful grimace.*] Are you okay?

DWAYNE [*smiling, unable to resist*]: My daughter's asking if her father is OK. [*Beat.*] Never mind me ... are you OK?

NAMHLA [*clearly not, still shaky*]: That was horrible … your wife.

DWAYNE [*considers this and gives a sad chuckle*]: I had a wife once. No ring … no vows … a marriage in all but name.

NAMHLA watches this man who wears his broken heart on his sleeve so openly. DWAYNE withdraws his bandaged hand from his side … they both notice the blood that appears to be oozing through the bandage.

NAMHLA [*startled*]: Oh, my God – your hand! It's bleeding!

DWAYNE [*wicked laugh*]: Ja, maybe I shoulda' had those blimmen stitches, hey.

He heads for the makeshift coffee table.

NAMHLA [*unconvinced, hugely concerned*]: That looks a lot worse than …

DWAYNE: Hang on, hang on. I want to show you something.

NAMHLA: At least let me take you to the hospital!

While she pleads with him to take notice of his wound he picks up the crate, revealing the magnificent rhino horn on the neatly folded hessian bag.

DWAYNE: Take a look at this.

As DWAYNE places the crate to one side the pain in his side causes him to gasp. He drops onto the car seat. The sight of the rhino horn derails NAMHLA and, sitting beside him, she doesn't notice as DWAYNE lifts his shirt to reveal his blood-soaked vest.

NAMHLA [*aghast, looking at the horn*]: Oh, my oath, it's the … that's the …!

DWAYNE: This is his headstone! [*He glances at the door.*] To hell with Boksburg Lake! [*He is triumphant.*] Gonna bury this beside Jonas on Blueberry Hill.

There is a pause. NAMHLA *opens her handbag to remove her car keys and suddenly stops, freezes …*

NAMHLA: I feel so stupid … my phone … [*She takes the phone from her bag.*] I've got pictures of my mother on my phone. Dozens of them …

DWAYNE [*hugely excited*]: Let me see …

NAMHLA [*preoccupied with her phone, is speedily accessing her photo gallery*]: Here she is.

As NAMHLA *shows him the first picture of her mother,* DWAYNE *cannot contain his joy at seeing the image of the woman who has haunted him for more than 40 years.*

DWAYNE [*ecstatic*]: That's her …! She looks so happy!

NAMHLA: We'd just arrived in England … [*She swipes the screen.*]

DWAYNE: And that's you! My little girl!

They look at each other. NAMHLA *places her hand on his, making a connection. Quietly, imperceptibly at first, comes the sound of the Soweto Gospel Choir singing the haunting 'Noyana' (Are you going there?).*

NAMHLA [*looking at him tenderly*]: Just to know … she was loved. [*She breaks eye contact and moves on.*] This one was taken at the New Forest …

DWAYNE [*fighting through the pain from the bullet wound in his side*]: Don't go so fast! [*She complies.*] Wait … let me see that one.

NAMHLA: I love this one.

DWAYNE [*beaming, awestruck*]: To see her smiling … just to see her smiling …

NAMHLA: She smiled a lot. [*Beat.*] My mother smiled, come rain or shine.

The full choir comes in, joining the solo. The music surges now, loud and powerful. As NAMHLA flicks the pictures of her late mother across the screen she becomes as entranced as the man beside her, completely unaware of his still-bleeding wound. DWAYNE leans back on the car seat.

The music swells … and swells. NAMHLA is smiling … DWAYNE's agony intensifies, yet his eyes remain locked on the pictures that flick across the smart phone screen.

We hold … the music soaring onward and upward … as lights slowly fade to …

BLACKOUT

Printed and bound by CPI Group (UK) Ltd, Croydon, CR0 4YY

14/04/2025

14656906-0001